CLASSIC **GUNS** OF THE **WORLD** SERIES

AMERICAN SUBMACHINE GUNS

1919–1950

AMERICAN SUBMACHINE GUNS
1919–1950

LUC GUILLOU

CLASSIC GUNS OF THE WORLD SERIES

THOMPSON SMG

M3 "GREASE GUN"

REISING

UD M42

ACCESSORIES

Schiffer Publishing Ltd

4880 Lower Valley Road • Atglen, PA 19310

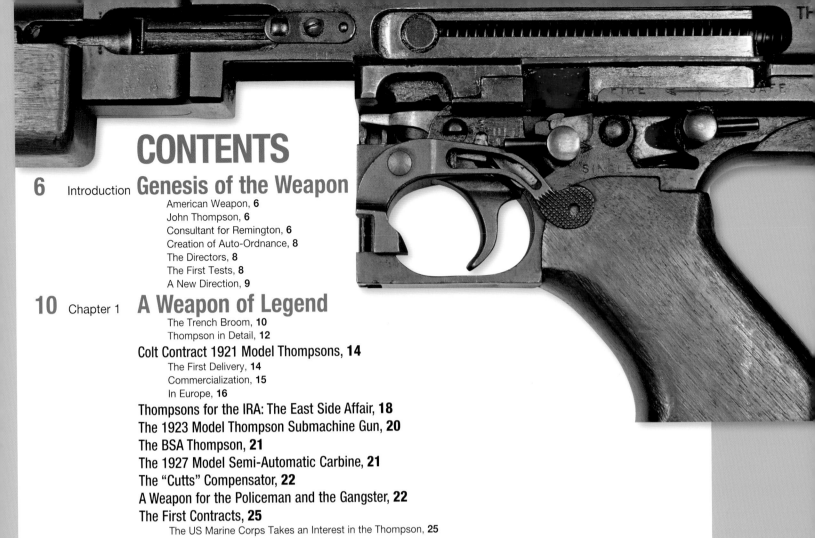

CONTENTS

GENESIS OF THE WEAPON

Gen. John Taliaferro Thompson. Born in 1860, graduated from West Point in 1882, became the youngest colonel in the United States army. Appointed as responsible for small caliber weapons in the headquarters of equipment in the US Army, he played a leading part in the development of the 1903 Springfield model rifle, and then presided over the adoption of the 1911 Colt model pistol. Having left the army around 1914, he was charged with setting up the Eddystone factory and organized the mass production of the US 17. Having perceived the necessity to arm the infantry with a compact and powerful weapon, he created a company to develop and commercialize this type of weapon: the Auto-Ordnance corporation. *DR*

It was summer 1918 and German Gen. Erich Ludendorff had just launched a great offensive by which he hoped to pierce the Allied front at the point where the French and British lines met. This operation, called "*Friedensturm*" (peace offensive), represented, for a Germany bled dry, the last hope of winning the war.

Germany was also placed in a difficult situation by the US entering the war in 1917. The size of the peacetime army was derisory, but the influx of volunteers rapidly turned it into a considerable force that began to harden to war while the overseas armaments industries increased in strength. This meant the Americans were able to fight with their own equipment (cannons, submachine guns, tanks) rather than equipment donated by France.

American Weapon

During the summer of 1918, American troops showed their prowess at Château-Thierry and Saint Mihiel. It was during these combats that they got acquainted with a new and redoubtable enemy weapon: the Bergmann MP18/1 submachine gun that proved to be admirably adapted to close-quarter combat. The Americans had only their light machine guns, and Winchester 1897 and 1912 model pump action shotguns: 12-caliber pump action shotguns whose redoubtable volleys of buckshot had no equal for sweeping a conquered trench or engaging in an enemy assault.

The use of these weapons, not in conformity with the Hague convention which forbade the use of non-jacketed projectiles, raised the strong indignation of the Germans, who threatened to shoot forthwith any American soldier caught with one of these weapons.

The American senior command chose therefore to withdraw the "trench guns" from the frontline and posted them to the rear, leaving its men without the weapon that was the equivalent of a German MP18/1.

John Thompson

In the United States a man who had been interested in the mechanisms of semi-automatic rifles for many years was on the point of conceiving the first American submachine gun. The man was a retired officer: John Taliaferro Thompson.

Born in 1860, graduated from West Point in 1882 to the Ordnance Corps, Thompson was not only a technician and an organizer; he was also a man of action.

He made his mark in Cuba during the Spanish–American War and concluded from this experience that the American army must reject all hand weapons of a caliber less than .45.

After the conflict, he nonetheless continued to affix the initials "JTT" on the .38 caliber Colt of which he ensured the supply for the US Army; he also piloted with energy a series of tests with the aim of adopting a new regulation hand weapon. He succeeded in imposing the choice of the .45 caliber Colt automatic pistol, which was to be adopted in 1911.

In 1909, he was named colonel at the age of forty-nine, making him the youngest of that rank in the American army.

Consultant for Remington

Five years later, Col. Thompson made a request to retire in order to work for the Remington company as a consultant engineer. Remington had to respond to a massive order for the P.14 placed in the US by Great Britain. From this period, Thompson advocated the idea that this production could be brought forward to supply the US government in the American caliber of .30-06 if the country should also have to enter the war. Thompson was tasked by Remington to set up a subsidiary which would be entirely dedicated to the manufacture of the P.14: the Eddystone company, that in two years Thompson would make into the largest manufacturer of light weapons in the world.

This remarkable success however left Thompson unsatisfied as he had a secret, unfulfilled ambition: to develop an automatic rifle for the American army.

The Colt 1911 was the most common close-quarter combat weapon in the American expeditionary force in Europe.

German MP18/1, the first submachine gun used in combat, entered the lists in 1918.

Weapons of an American soldier of the First World War: a 1903 Springfield, a US 17, a 1912 or 1897 Winchester trench gun, and hand weapons: 1911 Colt (not 1911 A1), and 1917 Colt revolver. *Collection of the Royal Army Museum of Brussels, photo by Marc de Fromont*

The Trench gun: 12-caliber pump-action rifle capable of short-range saturation fire but was not equal to the MP18 beyond a range of twenty-five meters.

It was in 1914, on the occasion of the wedding of his son, Cmdr. Marcellus Thompson officer of the coastal infantry, that Thompson met a businessman of Irish descent: Thomas Fortune Ryan, whose wealth had come from different sectors of industry.

His business affairs had put him in charge of a considerable amount of capital and Thomas F. Ryan was ready to invest in any domain likely to bring in a rapid and impressive return on investment. When Thompson was introduced to Ryan and shared his conviction that the semi-automatic rifle would be inevitably called on to replace the manual magazine rifle, the Irish-American businessman understood immediately that there were big profits to be made for the first company to come up with an operational weapon of this type.

Creation of Auto-Ordnance

As a result of this meeting Thomas Fortune Ryan suggested Thompson leave Remington in order to become an associate with him in an enterprise whose vocation was to develop and commercialize the semi-automatic rifle that had been in his mind for a long time.

Thompson and Ryan founded, on August 25, 1916, the "Auto Ordnance corporation." The terms "Auto," alluding to the automatic weapons and "Ordnance," designating regulation equipment in the US, clearly indicated the ambitions: to build an automatic weapon and have it adopted by the US Army. Several months later, the associates modified the name of their company. It was from then on referred to as "Auto-Ordnance Corporation."

During the tests of 1909, and while he was still serving in the Army, Thompson tasked a young technician in his service, Theodor Eickhoff, to carry out an inventory of the principal automatic rifle mechanisms presented to the US Army along with the main systems in service in the world.

This informative approach, particularly judicious, allowed Thompson to select the principles of operation that seemed to him to be the most pertinent. Amongst these, he was particularly interested by the ingenuity of a bolt invented by a US Navy frigate captain John Blish, who had discovered new properties of certain metals relating to adhesion; when machined at very specific angles, these metals became alternately adhesive or repellent depending on the pressure exerted on them. When applied to the breech of firearms this eliminated the need for lubrication, linkages and so on. Thompson considered this principle, initially designed for naval artillery parts, could be applied in a miniaturized version to the bolts of automatic rifles.

The Directors

When the Auto-Ordnance company was founded, the main sponsor Thomas Fortune Ryan and his lawyer, John Larkin, along with commander Blish, were among the main shareholders, who also included Thompson and his wife. Blish gave up the patent of the Blish locking system in exchange for a handsome portfolio of shares.

John Larkin took up his responsibility as director of the company while Thompson's son Marcellus was named vice president and general manager.

Shortly after the creation of the Auto-Ordnance company in 1916, Thompson hired Theodor Eickhoff whose great technical competence he much admired.

When the US entered the war in April 1917, the work of Thompson was suspended for a time and he was called up; he rejoined the ordnance corps command in Washington.

His son Marcellus, also called up, left to command an artillery regiment on the French front.

Despite the absence of Thompson, the development work of the new weapon went well under the drive of Theodor Eickhoff.

The First Tests

The tests of various prototypes took place in the research workshop that Auto-Ordnance set up in Cleveland in premises rented from the firm Warner & Swasey, well known amongst collectors for the marksman's goggles that they manufactured during the First World War for Springfield 1903 model rifles.

The technical team at Auto-Ordnance did not delay in creating several prototypes of automatic rifles with the Blish locking system (that will be referred to as semi-automatic if we choose to adopt post-1945 French regulation terminology). The operation of these weapons constantly ran into problems concerning the extraction of fired bullet casings, which only disappeared when the casings were lightly lubricated before use.

Eickhoff managed to carefully analyze the extraction process and showed that each type of round carried its own "extraction coefficient," which determined the force required to extract a cartridge, enlarged by firing, from the chamber.

Through a series of measures, Oscar V. Payne, another employee of Auto-Ordnance, brought to light the incompatibility between the high pressures created by the .30-06 rounds with the mechanisms of the breech with a Blish lock. Theodor Eickhoff gave a report of his findings to Thompson.

Even though he was inundated with work, Thompson followed attentively the development of the research carried out at Auto-Ordnance. He was fully aware of the difficulties of extraction encountered in the .30-06 prototypes. Consequently he was not surprised to learn of the conclusions arrived at by Payne.

Another attempt to increase the infantryman's firepower was the Pedersen conversion, which meant rounds very close to those that were to be used later on French 7.65 mm Long submachine guns could be fired in the Springfield 1903 modified A1 model. *DR*

Thomas Fortune Ryan. Irish by birth, this financier and associate of John T. Thompson was the principal backer of Auto-Ordnance. He was strongly suspected of having links with the traffic of Thompsons for the IRA. *DR*

A New Direction

Because of the responsibility that he held within the US Army Ordnance, Thompson was particularly well placed to analyze the situation and draw conclusions from it.

Two elements encouraged him to redirect the strategy of Auto-Ordnance:

- The recent adoption of the BAR (Browning Automatic Rifle), which constituted both a squad support weapon and an automatic rifle able to be used by a single man, meant that from then on it was highly unlikely that the US Army would carry out an effort to re-equip every man with another type of automatic rifle during war-time.

- The extraction coefficient of the .45 caliber round of the 1911 model Colt automatic pistol showed itself to be a lot more interesting than that of the .30 caliber 1906 model rifle (.30-06). Thus it seemed wiser to develop a weapon in this caliber if a successful conclusion was to be reached rapidly.

Thompson therefore ordered Eickhoff to shelve the current research on the automatic rifle and, with the help of Oscar Payne, to get started immediately on the development of a compact .45 caliber weapon, capable of continuous burst fire and equipped with a large capacity magazine: in other words, a submachine gun,

Presentation of the trench gun in the May 11, 1918 issue of *Scientific American*.

that Thompson named the "Trench Broom." Thompson insisted however that the Blish lock was kept on the new weapon.

Theodor Eickhoff. This young, talented technician played a decisive role in the development of the Thompson submachine gun.

American soldiers in France training with Browning Automatic Rifles in 1918.

CHAPTER 1

A WEAPON OF LEGEND

Cmdr. John Bell Blish, inventor of a locking system initially destined for artillery pieces, that was adapted to the breech of the first Thompson submachine guns. *DR*

From the month of September 1917, Theodor Eickhoff and Oscar Payne were in a position to send Thompson a working diagram of an eight-inch barrel weapon, christened "The Persuader": stripped of a butt, bearing a rear pistol grip and another under the barrel between which there was a receiver containing .45 ammunition. The Persuader was equipped with a delayed opening breech by Blish lock and with a fire mode selector positioned above the rear pistol grip, which enabled the choice of one of three options: safety, single shot fire, and continuous burst fire. The rate of the latter was almost 1,000 rounds per minute.

The Trench Broom

The principle of this weapon was approved by Thompson. Unfortunately the weapon was not definitively ready until November 1918.

When the armistice was signed, the US government backed out of the majority of current contracts with arms and military equipment manufacturers, thus the hopes that Auto-Ordnance entertained of seeing the Persuader adopted by the US Army collapsed.

Faced with this new situation, the main shareholders of Auto-Ordnance decided to pursue the development of the weapon, this time with the aim of supplying American police officers and also foreign governments.

It was also around this time that it was decided to abandon belted ammunition in order to answer Thompson's wishes of having a weapon that was both quick to reload and easy to handle, even in total darkness. The improved version of the Persuader was therefore equipped with a vertical 20-round magazine positioned on two interlocking columns and seen alternately on each lip of the magazine, as well as a simplified breech ensuring more reliability than the Persuader. This new version was called "Annihilator."

Even though they were still without a butt and sight mechanism, the various prototypes of the Annihilator already show the profile of the later Thompson submachine guns.

The last version, christened the Annihilator III, was considered sufficiently ready to be presented to police forces where Auto-Ordnance saw a favored client in peace time and during times of military credit restrictions.

To start making pre-production versions of the weapon, the company had to get equipped with more machine tools and hire more personnel. Through lack of space, the company had to move to another workshop site also in Cleveland.

The final version of the Annihilator, equipped with a round bolt face placed at the top of the receiver and a mobile firing pin, was called "Thompson Submachine gun model of 1919" and this name was conserved by the Auto-Ordnance board of directors as the designation of the weapon.

That same year, the Thompson 1919 model benefitted from a new modification which was to give it its definitive contour: the rear pistol grip was slightly repositioned nearer the front, so as to free a space under the receiver allowing a guideway to be fitted used to attach a removable butt to the weapon. The assembly of a butt, like those of the sight mechanisms, remains nonetheless exceptional on these pre-production versions.

The Sabin building workshop in Cleveland, Ohio, manufactured forty 1919 model or Annihilator type Thompson submachine guns. This number however is uncertain and many American historians are convinced that from between ten to twenty non-listed weapons, with the number erased, must have been produced secretly in order to be sent to the Irish Republican Army (IRA).

The "Persuader," prototype of a submachine gun with Blish lock, fed by a cartridge belt. *DR*

One of the various versions of the Thompson 1919 model. This prototype is already very close to the future 1921 model. It has neither a sight nor butt. At a later stage the rear grip would be moved nearer the front so as to allow the fitting of a butt assembly guideway. *DR*

An MP18/1 German submachine gun with its snail drum magazine, a Thompson 1921 submachine gun with its drum magazine, and a 1918 Browning. *Collection of the Royal Army Museum of Brussels, photo by Marc de Fromont*

THOMPSON IN DETAIL

First type of markings indicating the firing selector and safety catch markings "Automatic" and "Semi-automatic" highlighted with small arrows, as found on guns under serial no. 3000. Selector markings over serial 3000 read "Full Auto" and "Single" with a different style of arrows.

Second type of markings for the selector and safety catch.

The round bolt handle.

Left side marking of a Model 1921, serial no. 1887.

Lyman-made rear sight allowing a precise range and drift adjustment.

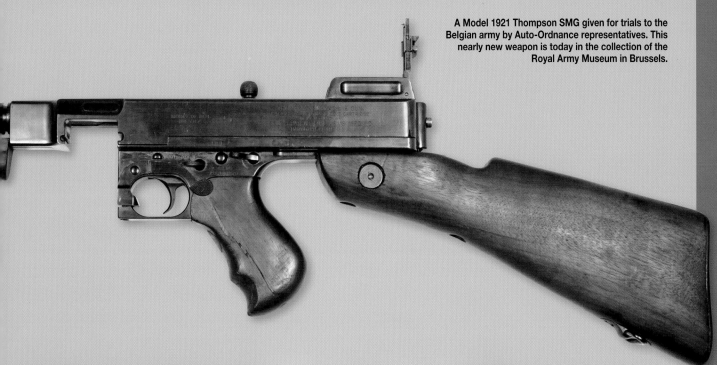

A Model 1921 Thompson SMG given for trials to the Belgian army by Auto-Ordnance representatives. This nearly new weapon is today in the collection of the Royal Army Museum in Brussels.

Guideway in front of the underframe where 50 or 100 round magazine can be fitted. The drum magazine is inserted from the left after locking the bolt rearward, safety catch on, and therefore preventing a firing accident.

The "L" marking on a drum magazine (a Roman numeral indicating a content of 50-rounds). The marking "Wind to 11 clicks" is a specific instruction for the slower model of 1928.

Feeding lips on an "L" drum magazine.

Rear view of an "L" magazine.

Front view of an "L" magazine showing the winding key. The arrows indicate the positioning rib for fitting on the underframe guideway.

One of the 15,000 1921 model Thompsons made by Colt between 1919 and 1921 for Auto-Ordnance.

COLT CONTRACT 1921 MODEL THOMPSONS

French language Auto-Ordnance publicity notice.

Despite the end of the war and still convinced that their weapon had commercial prospects the directors of Auto-Ordnance signed a contract, on August 18, 1920, with the Colt company for them to ensure the manufacture of 15,000 1919 type submachine guns. Commencing in March 1921, the manufacture of the Thompsons ordered by Auto-Ordnance would finish in July 1922.

The First Delivery

After the necessary time period to set up mass production, Colt delivered the first Thompson submachine gun to Auto-Ordnance on March 30, 1921.

This weapon, numbered in such a way as to follow on from those that had been previously made in the Cleveland workshop, received the serial number 41.

The first three specimens produced by Colt were still made according to the initial specifications of the 1919 model stipulated by the contract of August 18, 1920. They bore neither sight mechanisms nor a butt.

It was only after the first No. 45 specimen left the factory that Auto-Ordnance came to an agreement with Colt that a guideway be added under the receiver to permit the fixing of a removable butt and so that from then on the weapons delivered by Colt be equipped as standard with a Lyman sight adjustable up to 650 yards.

These modifications were the subject of an amendment to the initial contract and the modified version was designated "model 1921 A."

The wood was supplied by Remington Arms Co., the sight by the Lyman company, the preform casts of the receivers were forged by the Billings & Spencer Metalworks of Hartford, Connecticut. Colt carried out the machining, the final adjustments, the assembly, and the operation checks, along with the manufacture of the barrel.

These weapons could use straight 20-round magazines (magazine XX) as well as 50-round (magazine L) or 100-round (magazine C) drum magazines, identifiable in the catalogues by the Roman numerals "XX," "L," and "C."

The excessively light breech of the Annihilator, which gave the weapon an excessively high firing rate (in the order of 1,500 shots per minute!), was made heavier on the production series by doing away with the filing process on the lower side which served to lighten the weapon. This modification, associated with the positioning of a more flexible recoil spring, brought the firing rate to a more reasonable level (although still high) of 800 shots per minute.

New York address of Auto-Ordnance on the rear right side of the receiver.

Patents covering the different components of the 1921 model Thompson middle, right side of the receiver.

Colt manufacturer's markings, which identify the first 1921 and 1928 models in the middle of the receiver on the left side.

Initials JHB of Maj. John H. Barrett, former officer of US Army Ordnance responsible for final weapon inspections by Auto-Ordnance.

The breech, wide diameter recoil spring and its buffer pitot, Blish lock, and actuator of a 1921 model Thompson.

After the weapon bearing the serial number 3000 left the factory, the markings of the fire mode selector and Auto-Ordnance logo applied above the receiver were modified, whereas the forward end of the cocking handle groove, up until then machined in a square shape, was rounded. This was to avoid cracks forming as a result of the repeated impact of the cocking handle during firing on the angles in the first version.

Commercialization

As the majority of the technical questions had been resolved, Auto-Ordnance had simply to find buyers for the 15,000 submachine guns delivered by Colt.

The company explored an initial lead, to attempt to sell its submachine gun to the American military aviation as a ground to air weapon. The submachine guns, in a dual, fixed-wing installation were aimed at the ground so as to be used for spraying groups of enemy troops.

The assessment of the Thompson submachine gun by the US Army (military aviation was still under the responsibility of the US Army at that time), led to a reserved opinion as the testing commission stated, justifiably, that firing only automatic pistol rounds would always be inferior in terms of power, range, and accuracy than the onboard machine guns firing infantry rifle rounds.

Auto-Ordnance then carried out several promotion campaigns for its submachine gun with law enforcement organizations by systematically associating it with the motto (which was to be subsequently contradicted by the facts) "on the side of law and order."

Some supports enabling the weapon to be mounted on a motorcycle side car were proposed to the police.

First type Auto-Ordnance logo appearing at the top of the receiver on 1921 models bearing a number inferior to 3000.

Second model of the Auto-Ordnance logo, representing the signature of General Thompson in the outline of a bullet, which was to become definitively kept by the brand.

This stirrup-shaped piece, found inside the receiver on 1921 and 1928 models, has on both sides a felt pad whose function is to lubricate the breech during movement.

Some lead-loaded cartridges were proposed by Remington & Peters to respond to the demand of security firms that wished to use reduced-range projectiles, less likely to cause "collateral damage" in the case of confrontation in an urban environment. This cartridge was made of a paper bullet in a cal.45 ACP case with about 108 pellets of 7½ shot and effective up to fifty yards.

Later on a longer cartridge mounted with a multi-bullet projectile and containing large spherical buckshot placed on three lead discs was also marketed by Remington. Cartridges with longer casing, more powerful than that of the .45 ACP and christened ".45 Remington Thompson" were also tried out but without any further development.

In Europe

Still seeking military contracts, General Thompson and his demonstrator George E. Goll left for Europe to carry out a series of demonstrations of their weapon in military environments in Great Britain, France, Belgium, and Spain.

For the countries on the European continent General Thompson had taken the precaution of having several demonstration models made equipped with Lyman sights operating in meters and not in yards as on those of production models.

In every country Thompson visited, he encountered nothing more than polite curiosity. It was at the time when Thompson and George E. Goll were carrying out their demonstration tour that the *East Side* affair broke out and as such destroyed any sympathies the British had for this weapon and also was responsible for spreading a negative atmosphere around the Thompson.

Receiver seen from above showing the relative positions of the breech and its lubrication part, its recoil spring, and buffer pitot.

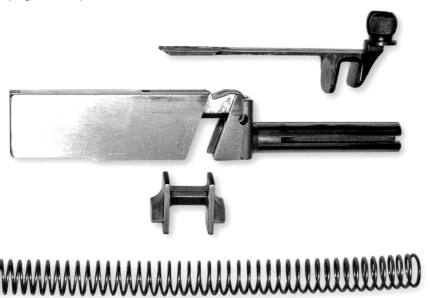

Detailed view of the breech, its lock and buffer pitot, and recoil spring of the 1921 model.

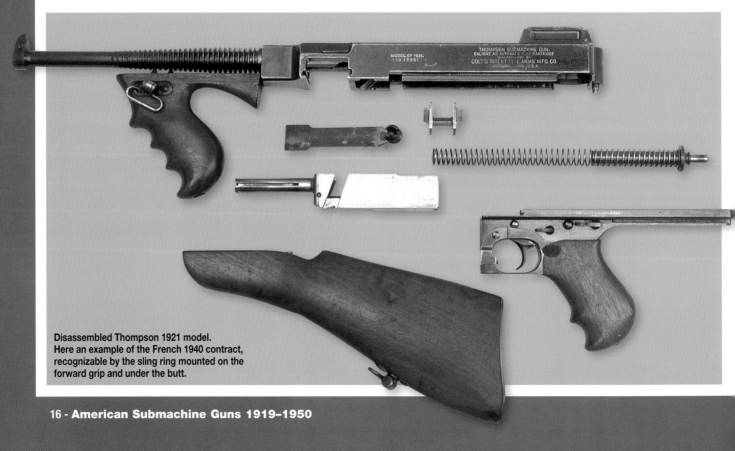

Disassembled Thompson 1921 model. Here an example of the French 1940 contract, recognizable by the sling ring mounted on the forward grip and under the butt.

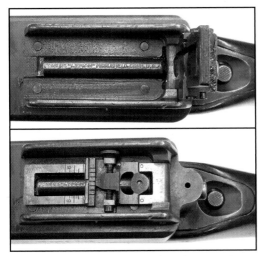

Lyman sight adjustable from 0 to 650 yards, mounted on 1921, 1928, and some 1928A1 models.

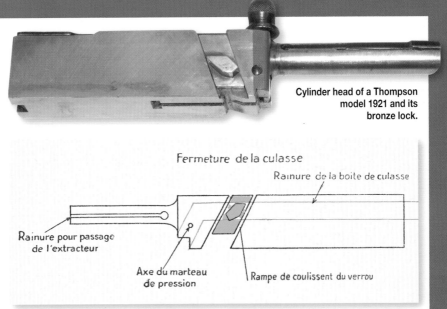

Cylinder head of a Thompson model 1921 and its bronze lock.

Fermeture de la culasse

Rainure de la boîte de culasse

Rainure pour passage de l'extracteur

Axe du marteau de pression

Rampe de coulissent du verrou

Diagram showing the breech in return phase to the front (closure). The lateral extensions of the Blish lock (in green) slide in the groove machined on the inside of the receiver (in red). They are on the point of reaching the zone where the groove on the receiver goes down diagonally frontwards. Being supported on the upper edge of the groove, the extensions force the lock-to drop, cusing in turn the breech to lock. *"Les pistolets et pistolets-mitrailleurs français et étrangers,"* 1952.

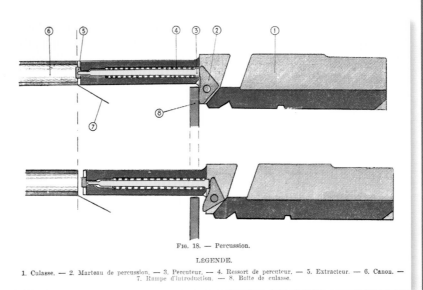

Fig. 18. — Percussion.

LÉGENDE.

1. Culasse. — 2. Marteau de percussion. — 3. Percuteur. — 4. Ressort de percuteur. — 5. Extracteur. — 6. Canon. — 7. Rampe d'introduction. — 8. Boîte de culasse.

Breech closing sequence.

Gen. John T. Thompson carrying out a demonstration of an early 1921 model, without the guideway to attach the butt. *DR*

A cam positioned at the bottom of the breech activates the firing pin when the breech closes.

Features of the 1921 Model Thompson	
Caliber	.45 (11.43 mm)
Ammunition	.45 ACP (Automatic Colt Pistol)
Total length	86 cm (92 cm for ones equipped with a "Cutts" compensator)
Barrel length	26.6 cm
Weight without magazine	4.53 kg
Weight with 20-round magazine	5.1 kg
Weight with 50-round magazine	6.7 kg
Rate of fire	Approx. 800 shots per minute

THOMPSONS FOR THE IRA: THE EAST SIDE AFFAIR

One of the 1921 model Thompson supplied to the IRA by American sympathizers of Irish origin with its 100-round magazine, which rendered the weapon heavy and cumbersome. *Photo by Yves L. Cadiou*

An Irish volunteer posing proudly with his 1921 model Thompson and its "C" magazine.

Small poster that the IRA put in public telephone boxes to warn callers of the danger of telephone tapping. The watchword of the IRA "Whatever you say, say nothing," could still prove useful today among arms collectors!

In June 1921, 495 Thompson 1921 models which had been covertly put on board the SS *East Side* were seized by New York customs.

These submachine guns, along with other weapons, were destined for the Irish Republican Army (IRA), an underground organization fighting against the British presence in Ireland. On the majority of these weapons the serial number had been removed with a welding torch to reduce traceability.

Thomas Fortune Ryan, the sponsor of Auto-Ordnance, who was a personal friend of the Irish president Aemon de Valera and maintained a number of relationships within Irish independence organizations set up in the US, was strongly suspected of having personally financed the purchase of several hundred Thompsons for the IRA behind the scenes.

The investigation, led by a promising young policeman called John Edgar Hoover (future head of the FBI [Federal Bureau of Investigation]) established that an initial, smaller delivery of Thompsons had already reached Ireland where the weapons had been used in various skirmishes with British forces.

The load seized on board the SS *East Side* constituted a violation of the laws of neutrality decreed in the US during the First World War which prohibited the movement of arms from the United States to countries at war.

Although it is almost certain that Thomas Fortune Ryan played an active part in this arms trafficking affair, Thompson and his son Marcellus were also suspected of having turned a blind eye to these purchases.

The abolition in 1921 of the laws of neutrality adopted during the First World War along with the abandonment of legal proceedings undertaken by the British Crown against Auto-Ordnance due to the return of peace to Ireland in 1922, meant the directors of Auto-Ordnance avoided any legal action.

It seems that two other covert deliveries of Thompsons took place in Ireland after the signature of the peace treaty of 1922. Among these weapons were not only the first 1921 models but also some rare 1919 models.

While the *East Side* affair was still ongoing, Auto-Ordnance pursued its efforts to try to interest diverse types of buyers for its weapon:

- The police forces to whom the weapon was proposed in various versions with multiple accessories: Cutts compensator limiting lift during continuous burst fire, transport cases, etc.

- Foreign armies to which Thompson proposed two new versions:
  - The "1923 model," able to be chambered in various calibers (.45 ACP, 9 mm Bergmann-Bayard, 7.63 Mauser, .351 SL), fitted with a bipod and able to receive a bayonet.
  - A light version in 9 mm Parabellum: the manufacture was to be carried out in Great Britain at BSA and the outline was more in keeping with the European way. This variation never got beyond the pre-production stage.

The individual market was not forgotten and a version only capable of single shot fire, the 1927 semi-automatic Thompson rifle, was added to the catalogue.

On this Thompson delivered to the IRA, the serial number has been hastily removed by welding torch. *Pattern Room Enfield, photo by Yves L. Cadiou*

Loose-talk costs lives
In taxis
On the phone
In clubs and bars
At football matches
At home with friends
Anywhere!
Whatever you say - say nothing

Several weapons used during the Irish civil war: a 1921 model Thompson fitted with a 50-round drum magazine ("L" drum) and on the left a 100-round drum magazine ("C" drum), a Lewis light machine gun, and a Lee-Metford rifle of the Irish constabulary. *Collection of the Royal Army Museum of Brussels, photo by Marc de Fromont*

THE 1923 MODEL THOMPSON SUBMACHINE GUN

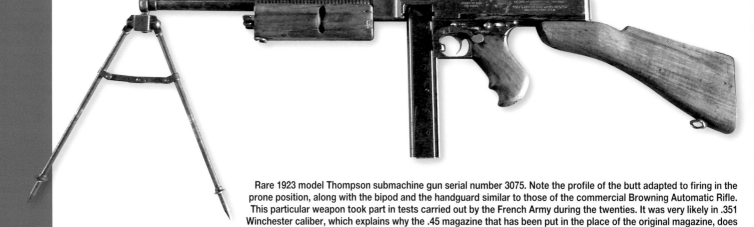

Rare 1923 model Thompson submachine gun serial number 3075. Note the profile of the butt adapted to firing in the prone position, along with the bipod and the handguard similar to those of the commercial Browning Automatic Rifle. This particular weapon took part in tests carried out by the French Army during the twenties. It was very likely in .351 Winchester caliber, which explains why the .45 magazine that has been put in the place of the original magazine, does not take up all the space as the original magazine was much bigger.
Collection Musée de l'Armée, photo by Jacques Barlerin

Weapon with folded bipod. *Collection Musée de l'Armée, photo by Jacques Barlerin*

Even though this is theoretically a 1923 model, the receiver of the weapon in fact bears the marking "model of 1921." *Collection Musée de l'Armée, photo by Jacques Barlerin*

This test bore the evidence of a wrong strategic decision on the part of Auto-Ordnance and was without consequence. It consisted of proposing a "light support weapon" by equipping the Thompson submachine gun with a bipod which, associated with the Lyman sight and a butt adapted for firing in the prone position meant the Thompson 1923 model submachine gun could pass for a support weapon. However, the ballistic performance of the pistol cartridges used by this weapon was clearly insufficient to think it could compete with real light machine guns firing rifle rounds.

The only asset of the 1923 model Thompson compared with traditional light machine guns was its lightness but that was insufficient to arouse the interest of the military authorities.

An attempt to propose a transformed version to fire more powerful rounds: the .351 Winchester did not have more success. One of these weapons was tested between 1924 and 1926 by the French Army and fortunately one of these test specimens is conserved today in one of its technical establishment collections.

Left: a .45 ACP cartridge, and right: a .351 SL cartridge. *Photo by Jacques Barlerin*

The 1923 model Thompson used as a support weapon. It is this "light machine gun" capability which justified the fixing of a sight as elaborate as the Lyman sight on a submachine gun. *Auto-Ordnance*

THE BSA THOMPSON

Several European countries expressed an interest in the Thompson chambered in 9 mm Parabellum and so Thompson took the necessary steps to propose the production of such a weapon under license with the British firm BSA.

BSA accepted this proposition and, from 1926, manufactured a small number of submachine guns which kept the internal mechanism of the Thompson but the outward aspect was restyled to conform more with European norms and gave them the appearance of small, semi-automatic rifles. The weapon was tested by both Belgium and France. The weapons archive in Chatellerault, France, still have the reports of the tests carried out in 1927 by the technical establishment at Versailles (ETVS) on this weapon.

Other specimens manufactured in .45 Colt automatic, 9 mm Bergmann Bayard, and 7.63 mm Mauser were presented to different European countries.

However the time had not yet come for the armies of the old continent to consider the submachine gun as none other than a cut-rate light machine gun or a police weapon (or even a gangster weapon). The manufacture of this European version of the Thompson by BSA stopped therefore at the end of the twenties. This weapon is quite rare today and is largely only found in museums.

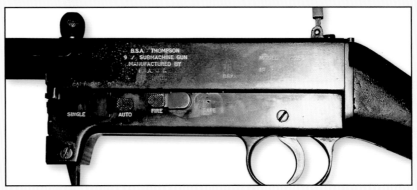

Marking on a BSA Thompson. *Photo by Wolf Riess*

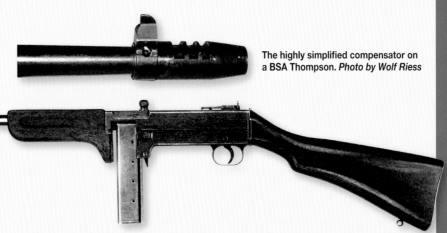

The highly simplified compensator on a BSA Thompson. *Photo by Wolf Riess*

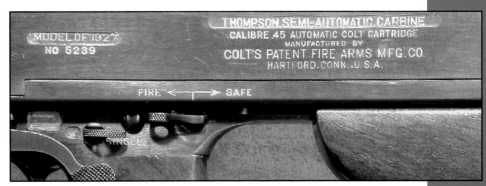

British BSA made Thompson in 9 mm Parabellum caliber. This photo appeared in a French Army test report. *CAA*

THE 1927 MODEL SEMI-AUTOMATIC CARBINE

Unlike the previous weapon, this was a version only allowing semi-automatic fire (single shot) developed for sale to individuals and possibly to police forces and prison guards. The number of 1927 model Thompsons manufactured was very limited and this model represents the dream of a great many Thompson collectors. To date, only forty-seven original semi-automatic 1927 model carbines are listed in the world. It is evident that the period models should not be confused with the weapons commercialized after the war under the same name by the Numrich Arms Co.

The 1927 models arise from the transformation of the 1921 model Thompson, whose markings were modified as a consequence:

A re-engraved model after the "model of 1921," marked on the original receiver, had been removed. The indication "Full Auto" (continuous burst fire) unnecessary on this weapon has been filed off. Marking "Thompson Semi-Automatic Carbine" replacing the original inscription "Thompson submachine gun." *www.gunauction.com*

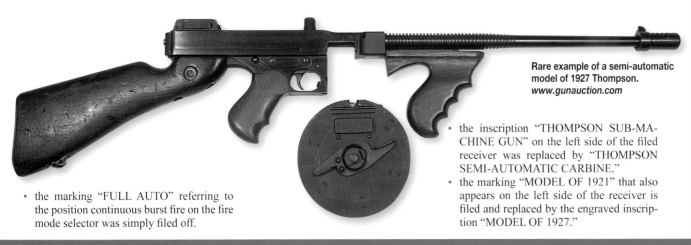

Rare example of a semi-automatic model of 1927 Thompson. *www.gunauction.com*

- the marking "FULL AUTO" referring to the position continuous burst fire on the fire mode selector was simply filed off.

- the inscription "THOMPSON SUB-MA-CHINE GUN" on the left side of the filed receiver was replaced by "THOMPSON SEMI-AUTOMATIC CARBINE."
- the marking "MODEL OF 1921" that also appears on the left side of the receiver is filed and replaced by the engraved inscription "MODEL OF 1927."

THE "CUTTS" COMPENSATOR

This accessory was to play an important role in the history of the Thompson by increasing its stability during bursts of automatic fire and thereby improve its accuracy. It is a muzzle brake conceived by Col. Richard M. Cutts and his son; Lt. Richard M. Cutts Jr.

The compensator, screwed to the muzzle of the weapon, causes some of the combustion gases to go upwards due to a series of slots machined on its upper side. This flow of gas counters the natural raising of the weapon during automatic firing.

Cutts and his son had initially conceived the compensator for the Browning automatic rifle. The Army did not adopt it but it was fitted on the "Monitor," a commercial version of the Browning used by some police forces and the FBI.

The version designed for the Thompson succeeded in improving accuracy by 140% on a 1921 model during automatic firing.

The Cutts compensator was not mounted as standard on the 1921 model, or rather the model 1921 A (as the version fitted with a butt and sight mechanisms was called), but it could be fitted as an option by request for $25.

The Thompson model of 1921 fitted with a compensator was designated as 1921 AC model in the catalogues of the period.

Subsequently, the Cutts compensator would be systematically fitted on the 1928 "Navy model," as well as on the 1928 and 1928A1 made during the Second World War. There are several variations of markings and slots in existence (different widths and arrangements). The Cutts compensator was made by the Lyman Company.

Just like the Thompson weapons, the Cutts compensators often carried an abundance of markings, the different variations bringing great joy to collectors.

Thanks to the Cutts compensator and its weight, the Thompson submachine gun 1921 model was controllable during bursts of automatic firing and auto shoulder firing, and even someone not very familiar with firing weapons could easily manage to group fifty shots fired from a drum magazine at a distance of fifty yards in a one square yard target. The results were even better with a 1928 model Thompson, with a rate of fire 200 shots per minute less compared to the 1921 model, that made shooting easier.

In semi-automatic fire, the fifty cartridges of the drum magazine could be fired with accuracy in less than thirty seconds.

A 1928 Auto-Ordnance advertisement showing the 1921 A model (standard) for $175 and the AC model fitted with a Cutts compensator for $25 more.

A WEAPON FOR THE POLICEMAN AND THE GANGSTER

Capt. Lutz of the New York police examines a 1921 model Thompson. *DR*

Between 1920 and 1930, the representatives of the Auto-Ordnance company travelled to small towns across the United States to present their submachine gun to local police forces.

When Auto-Ordnance authorized a new representative, the company supplied him with an advice booklet titled *How to Sell Thompson Anti-Bandit Guns*.

It also insisted to its salesmen that the sale of these weapons be reserved to buyers who were "on the side of law and order."

The salesmen were advised to present the weapon to the local police authorities and convince them that although it could not replace the revolver or pistol in daily use, it was the ideal tool for isolated patrols where the risk of confronting a group of adversaries was high, and also for routine road checks, during which .45 projectiles presented a higher probability of stopping a vehicle.

By the accuracy of its firing, the Thompson also reduced the risk of causing "collateral damage" common with hunting rifles. Even though this latter argument remains debatable, Auto-Ordnance succeeded in placing one or two submachine guns in every municipal police station.

Some weapons commonly used by American gangsters during the twenties: a 1921 model Thompson, a Winchester Riot Gun 1897 model, and a Colt and Smith and Wesson revolver .45 caliber 1917 model. Despite the fact that the last three weapons mentioned come from war surplus and were available at a cheap price, the Thompson was a heavy "investment": it was sold at the time by Auto-Ordnance for $200, the equivalent of a Ford Model T. The arms traffickers who supplied the underworld did not hesitate to ask ten times this price! *Collection of the Royal Army Museum of Brussels, photo by Marc de Fromont*

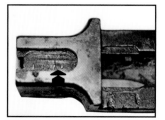

The armorers of the mob erased the serial numbers on the Thompsons that they managed to get hold of, so Colt transferred the serial number to the rear section of the barrel on the first 1,000 made and then to the grip support housing: a position which is only accessible once the barrel has been disassembled from the weapon.

In addition to the police, the Thompson was also sold to numerous bank and warehouse security organizations.

Unfortunately for Auto-Ordnance, some unscrupulous representatives did not hesitate to sell submachine weapons to members of organized crime.

The reputation of the Thompson submachine gun suffered slightly because of the sales made to the IRA, but above all its use by the American mob which gave it a very bad reputation.

The Volstead Act came into force in October 1919 prohibiting the sale of alcohol throughout the United States. This law opened the door to the highly lucrative trafficking of alcohol.

The division of territories and considerable profits that the trafficking generated led to many vendettas between rival gangs. These bloody confrontations, along with the necessity of protecting their storage depots and transport networks from the police, spurred the gangsters to arm themselves heavily.

Unlike soldiers and police officers who were unclear as to exactly what use to assign to these Thompson submachine guns, the gangsters understood immediately how this compact weapon with great firepower could be best put to use.

Manhunt in the Woolworth Tower in New York in 1936. Police armed with Thompsons and Remington Model 8s look for a villain inside the building. *DR*

John Edgar Hoover, boss of the FBI, with a Thompson model of 1921 or model of 1928 fitted with a Cutts compensator and a forward vertical grip. Hoover transformed the FBI into a highly effective tool to fight against organized crime between the wars, then into a counter-espionage organization during the Second World War. After the war, he led the fight against communist corruption in the United States and chased communist agents who infiltrated the country.

After Hoover had bought a pair of 1921 model Thompsons with his own funds in order to allocate them to two of his more at-risk agents, the "bureau" acquired several hundred 1921 and 1928 model Thompsons. Two special agents can be seen here at firing practice at the FBI academy at Quantico, Virginia. *Los Angeles Herald*

In 1930, Auto-Ordnance sent a circular to all its representatives forbidding them from that point on to make any sale to individuals.

Auto-Ordnance hoped in this way to learn the identity of the buyers and stop the weapons getting into the hands of the mob. As can be imagined, the miscreants rapidly circumvented this situation.

To face up to the over-arming of the mob, the various state police forces also purchased Thompsons, as well as the prison administration. The FBI, created in 1908 and taken over by J. Edgar Hoover in 1924, along with the Coast Guard also followed this example much to the satisfaction of Auto-Ordnance.

A squad of police officers armed with Thompsons. *DR*

THE FIRST CONTRACTS

The first significant official contract to benefit Auto-Ordnance curiously enough did not come from either the Army or the police but from the Postal Service. With the rise of crime in the United States after the First World War, postal employees were very often the target of armed attacks.

In 1926, following an attack which took the lives of several of its employees, the director of the Postal Service requested that from then on the government use US Marines to protect its transportations of cash. To enable the valiant Marines engaged in this mission to respond effectively to these attacks, the US Postal Service purchased 200 model 1921 Thompsons from Auto-Ordnance. The appointment of elite soldiers in a police activity could only be effective if they were granted war-time close-quarter fire rules of engagement. In the United States of the 1920s, the Marines probably received the order to open fire first when faced with any threat. The fact remains that their presence rapidly stopped attacks on postal convoys.

A picture from an Auto-Ordnance catalog showing a Marine armed with a Thompson watching over mail bags.

The US Marine Corps Takes an Interest in the Thompson

The Marines, having discovered and appreciated the Thompson during their mission for the Postal Service, considered that this weapon could be useful in guerilla and hand-to-hand combat and as such refrained from giving back the Thompsons to the Postal Service and took them when they were engaged in Mexico, Nicaragua, and ensuring the protection of international concessions in China.

In the hands of these tough combatants, the Thompson started to solidify its reputation as a military weapon.

Highly satisfied with the Thompson used for the Postal Service, the Marine Corps, which benefitted from a great independence concerning the choice of its weapon, decided to acquire several hundred Thompsons fitted with Cutts compensators to equip its various expeditionary forces.

The feedback and sharing of experience from the combatants was extremely positive and the only criticism of the weapon concerned its excessively high firing rate.

The use of the Thompson by the Marine Corps was the cause of the adoption of an accessory, very rare today: a small metal box opening like a glasses case, in which a brass pullthrough and brush, a chamber brush, and various spare parts (hammer with pin, firing pin, extractor, ejector) were placed. This box, made by the Worcester Pressed Steel Company based on the model that the firm already manufactured for the Smith and Wesson "Straight Line," had the same dimensions as a 20-round Thompson magazine and in this way could be easily transported in the central compartment of the magazine pouch. However the Marines preferred to carry it in their haversack and conserve their full supply of five 20-round magazines in case of difficulty!

This photo shows a Marine examining the remains of a Japanese soldier. The 50-round drum magazine was still occasionally used in combat in the Pacific. *DR*

This photo taken in the Pacific theatre illustrates perfectly the rapid firing speed and the excellent stability of the Thompson; the clarity of the image here proving the weapon scarcely moves as two ejected cases fly above it. *DR*

CHAPTER 2

1928 AND 1928A1 THOMPSONS

Thompson US Navy model of 1928. *Champlin Museum, photo by Allan Gruening*

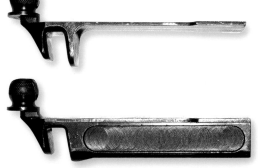

U.S. NAVY
MODEL OF 1928
NO 10398

THOMPSON SUBMACHINE GUN.
CALIBRE .45 AUTOMATIC COLT CARTRIDGE
MANUFACTURED BY
COLT'S PATENT FIRE ARMS MFG.CO
HARTFORD, CONN., U.S.A.

FIRE ◄——————► SAFE

Detail of the markings specific to the Thompson 1928 model supplied by Colt to the US Navy. The number "8" has overwritten the figure "1" on the initial marking "model of 1921." *Champlin Museum, photo by Allan Gruening*

Right: Above, a Thompson 1921 model bolt handle, below, the bolt handle weighted to slow the firing speed on a model 1928A1. While this piece was made from a single bloc on the 1928A1, it was composed of a heavy piece of steel welded to the 1921 model bolt handle on the US Navy 1928 model.

The 1928 US Navy Model

Taking into account the criticisms of the Marines concerning the weapon, the US Navy asked Auto-Ordnance to supply it with Thompsons modified so that the firing rate was reduced from 800 to around 600 rounds per minute.

To carry this out the large diameter recoil spring of the initial 1921 model was replaced by a smaller diameter spring; the diameter of the pitot was also reduced in proportion and the bolt handle was made heavier. A buffer system was added to the rear of the recoil spring.

Initially, Auto-Ordnance avoided manufacturing new bolt handles but only had a block of steel machined based on a design by Thomas V. Payne. This block was riveted and welded underneath the bolt handle on the 1921 model to increase their weight.

The Thompsons ordered by the Marines were fitted with a Cutts compensator and a horizontal handguard as well as two sling swivels. They took the name "US Navy model of 1928."

The unsold stocks of 1921 models being sufficient to satisfy the order for 500 submachine guns placed by the US Navy, the 1928 models, "US Navy model," were made from the 1921 model and the bolt handles, breech, recoil spring, and the pitot on this were replaced by parts from the new model and the figure "1" on the marking "model of 1921" was overwritten by a figure 8.

The wording "US NAVY" was stamped above the marking "MODEL OF 1928."

The 500 weapons purchased by the navy represented a fairly modest deal but it was widely taken advantage of by Auto-Ordnance in terms of advertising. Company catalogs immediately presented the model with reduced firing speed, horizontal handguard, and a Cutts compensator as the "US Navy model." A weapon of this type, sold commercially, was adorned with the marking US NAVY identical to that on the weapons delivered to the navy.

The weapons delivered to the Navy were fitted with 20-round vertical magazines or 50-round drum magazines. To take into account the less rapid firing rate on the 1928 model a new type of 50-round magazine was brought in.

On the Thompson 1921 model, which had a firing speed of 800 shots per minute, the key positioned at the front of the receiver of the drum magazine had to be wound to 11 clicks to transmit the correct tension to the recoil spring for this firing speed.

On the 1928 model Thompson winding to 9 clicks was enough for a firing rate of 600 shots per minute. For this reason, the marking "wind to 11 clicks" stamped on the forward of the drum magazines was replaced by the inscription "wind to 9 or 11 clicks" stipulating switching to 9 clicks for the 1928 model, and 11 clicks to the 1921 model.

T he Navy manifested their interest for the new Thompson submachine guns used by the Marines very rapidly. This weapon seemed to have an obvious appeal to arm the landing parties on war ships as well as the men on gunboats patrolling the rivers in China and the coastal areas in the Philippines.

This young Coast Guard accompanied by his dog with a 1928A1 model Thompson of a later make than the 1928 models initially supplied by Colt to the US Navy. The weapon appears to have a semi-matt finish and its very square forward handguard is slightly different from the one seen on the Colt 1928A1 US Navy. *DR*

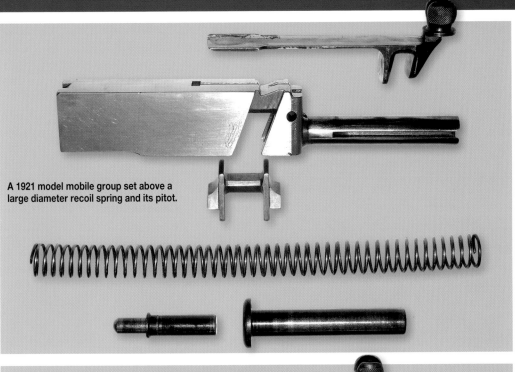

A 1921 model mobile group set above a large diameter recoil spring and its pitot.

Detail of a US 17 type sling ring mounted on the Navy models. *Champlin Museum, photo by Allan Gruening*

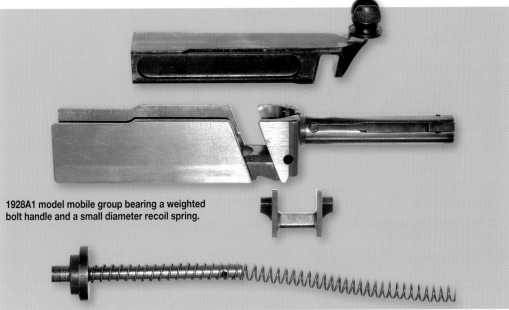

1928A1 model mobile group bearing a weighted bolt handle and a small diameter recoil spring.

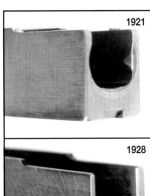

1921

1928

The cut of the rear of the bolt differs slightly between the 1921 and the 1928 model.

Two female Marine auxiliaries (perhaps dressed a little too nicely to carry out this dirty job) cleaning various service weapons including a Thompson M1 and Colt and Smith & Wesson revolvers. *DR*

Thompson Submachine Guns for the US Cavalry

Between the world wars, the US Cavalry began to abandon the use of horses, as all cavalries in the world, in favor of motorcycles and armored vehicles. It was in this context that the US Cavalry decided, in 1931, to issue one Thompson submachine gun per armored vehicle.

These weapons were of the same type as those adopted by the Navy but did not bear of course the marking "US NAVY."

The adoption of the Thompson submachine gun by the US Navy and the US Marine Corps was an important stage in the career of the weapon.

The adoption of the weapon by the Cavalry permitted Auto-Ordnance to get a foothold in the supplies system of the US Army and gave the weapon a "military legitimacy" that it had been seeking for a long time.

This success remained modest however and sales still did not reimburse the sum owed to Colt for the manufacture of the 15,000 "model of 1921" Thompsons, of which many remained unsold seven years later.

The US Cavalry adopted the Thompson a little before its general entry into service in the US Army. US Army Air Force recruits can be seen here in 1942 learning the basics of using a Thompson at the Mitchell Base in New York state. *DR*

This picture of a motorcyclist firing a Thompson protected by his motorcycle constitutes an optimistic vision of combat that the press hastened to circulate. *DR*

A lineup of proud motorcyclists, Thompsons aloft, at the beginning of the Second World War. This was taken up as a publicity picture by the Harley Davidson company whose motorcycles equipped the US Army. *DR*

Thompson submachine guns 1928 and 1928A1 model, 1918 Browning Automatic Rifle, and a Colt 1911 A1 model bestowed a great fire power to Marine detachments engaged in Latin America and China. *Collection of the Royal Army Museum of Brussels, photo by Marc de Fromont*

New Team, New Policy

The death of Thomas Fortune Ryan in November 1928, whose funds had guaranteed the durability of the company until that point despite its deficit, was a hard blow for the company.

Walter B. Ryan, a nephew of the deceased, replaced him as the president of the company. The team of directors was entirely changed.

From 1932, the new team imposed a new marketing policy forbidding its representatives from selling Thompsons to non-military users.

Subsequently, the new directors of Auto-Ordnance understood the risks involved in doing without clientele of the forces of order. So in 1932 they signed an agreement with the Federal Laboratory company of Pittsburgh which was assigned with Thompson sales outside the military sector.

This measure simply preempted the adoption which, two years later, forbad the ownership and the sale of automatic weapons to individuals.

For all that, the taking up of the Thompson submachine gun by the United States Army in 1938 did not save the situation because, in peacetime, the American Army was very small. The US Army order however concerned 15,000 corresponding to the US Navy model but marked "Submachine Gun M 1928A1." It seemed that the marking A1 (for Alteration No.1) included the adoption of a new model of ejector made in two parts and not one, as on previous models.

When Auto-Ordnance received this order in 1938, it had just concluded the sale of 4,100 Thompsons to foreign governments, and 4,700 to the United States and police forces and services.

This meant therefore that, of the 15,000 "model of 1921" Thompsons manufactured in 1921 and 1922 by Colt for Auto-Ordnance, 10,300 had been sold at that date, whereas 4,750 weapons were still in stock more than sixteen years after their production.

The Auto-Ordnance company only survived because of the injections of cash made by the Ryan family. As a consequence the inheritors of Thomas Fortune Ryan showed themselves to be keen to split from this loss-making company.

Russel Maguire, seen here holding a presentation model of a Thompson M1A1. *DR*

In 1939, Marcellus Thompson, who was still at that time the vice president of Auto-Ordnance, managed to convince the businessman Russel Maguire, to take over the company.

During negotiations, Marcellus Thompson suffered a stroke and died a short time later. His death was closely followed by that of his father, John T. Thompson, who died on June 21, 1940.

In May 1939, Russel Maguire had a new company named "Thompson Automatic Arms Corporation" registered in the state of New York. After the purchase of Auto-Ordnance Corporation by Russel Maguire, this company, whose only role had been to facilitate the assumption of power, merged with Auto-Ordnance and was officially dissolved in October 1941.

A shrewd and tenacious businessman, Russel Maguire had foreseen that the constant worsening in international relations was likely to lead to a major conflict which would open up prospects for the Thompson submachine gun. Indeed, orders started arriving at Auto-Ordnance from Great Britain, France, Sweden, and Yugoslavia at the end of 1939.

The Thompson submachine gun was the only tried and tested weapon of this type that was both available in number and not made in an Axis country (Germany or Italy).

TRADE MARK
Thompson

The "Tommy Gun"

Thompson Submachine Gun

SPECIFICATIONS of Model 28-AC

Caliber .45. Weight 9 lbs., 13 oz. Length 33 in. Length of barrel with Compensator 12½ in.; without Compensator, 10½ in. Equipped with Lyman sights and wind gauge. 20 and 50 cartridge capacity magazines. Ammunition, caliber .45 Colt Automatic Pistol Ball Cartridges (230-grain bullet). Cutts Compensator attached to muzzle of gun shown) increases rapidity and accuracy of semi-automatic fire, lessens tendency of muzzle rising in full-automatic firing and reduces recoil to practically nothing.

Auto-Ordnance Corporation

1437 Railroad Ave. Bridgeport, Conn.

Indispensable in Modern Warfare

Publicity leaflet for a Thompson 1928 AC model (model with compensator). The Railroad Avenue, Bridgeport address indicates it was made by Auto-Ordnance at Bridgeport, Connecticut. In spite of what the directors of the company would have people believe, Auto-Ordnance only made the receivers and the frame groups of its Thompsons. The barrels were made by Remington and many other parts were supplied by sub-contractors. However, a good control of the sub-contractors guaranteed the total interchangeability between parts made by Auto-Ordnance and those produced by Savage.

CHAPTER 3

THE THOMPSON AT WAR

A superb Colt-made Thompson delivered to the French Army in 1940.

The French Order of 1940

In 1939, the French government dispatched a purchasing assignment to the US tasked with acquiring rifles, submachine guns, light machine guns, tanks, and planes.

It was in this context that an order for several thousand Thompson 1921 model submachine guns was placed to Auto-Ordnance by the French government.

The 1935 Neutrality Act forbad American enterprises from selling armaments to any country at war. However some astute legal minds dug up a legal clause dating from the civil war which enabled this law to be bypassed: "Cash and Carry."

The French Army knew this weapon very well as they had tested Thompson .45 and .351 SL caliber in 1926 and the following year had carried out an assessment of a BSA made Thompson in 9 mm Parabellum.

Even though the French technical services did not recommend the adoption of the Thompson submachine gun at the time, the French Army had to revisit its position when its troops found themselves confronted with German adversaries well-equipped with submachine guns during the "Phony War" of 1939–40. However, the MAS 38 submachine gun, recently adopted by France, had just entered the mass production phase.

The French commission placed an order for 3,750 of the 1921 model Thompsons along with thirty million .35 cartridges, and took the option on 3,000 further Thompsons for a later purchase.

With war approaching, the Thompson submachine gun, which since 1921 had been so difficult to sell, was from now the object of many orders from Yugoslavia, Sweden, and soon Great Britain.

An order for 500 1928 AC (with Cutts compensator) Thompsons, placed in the name of the Swedish government in January 1940 by the AB Uno Lindholm Co., emptied the stocks of Colt-made Thompsons.

A French user guide for the 1921 model Thompson submachine gun published by Charles Lavauzelle in 1942 for the armistice army, the police, and mobile reserve groups. A second edition was to be published in 1944 just before the Liberation.

Surrounded by a cordon of guards armed with 1921 model Thompsons and MAS 36 rifles, a group of German prisoners cross the streets of Paris for captivity in 1944. *DR*

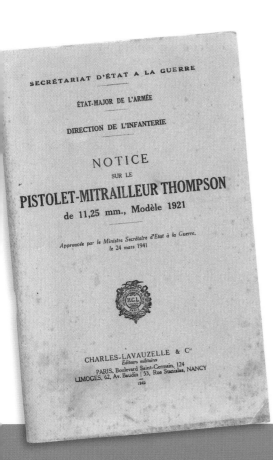

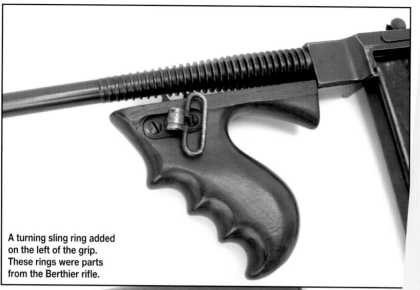

A turning sling ring added on the left of the grip. These rings were parts from the Berthier rifle.

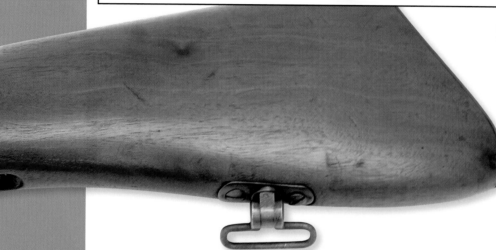

Turning sling ring added under the butt of its Thompson 1921 model by the French Army.

A certain number of Thompson model of 1921 seized from the French Army showed up in German weapons inventories under the name MP 721.

These weapons were made by converting Colt made 1921 model Thompsons to 1928 AC standards. The Swedish contract submachine guns were fitted with sights graduated in meters and the receiver was marked "model of 1928A1" by overwriting the "8" and "A1" stamped on the initial marking "Model of 1921." They were designated as Kpist m/40 in the Swedish army.

Soon after the French and Swedish orders were sent, the US Army ordered 951 model of 1928A1 Thompsons from Auto-Ordnance.

This American military order, which would have been much welcomed by Auto-Ordnance a few years earlier, came just at the time when the French, Swedish, and Yugoslavian orders had exhausted the remainder of 1921 model Thompsons.

Russel Maguire was well aware that the long-awaited market would escape Auto-Ordnance if the company was not able to respond quickly.

The Colt company was already monopolized by other military orders (1911 A11 model pistols, Browning .30 and .50 machine guns, etc;) so Maguire went to see one of the largest manufacturers of American weapons: the Savage Arms Corporation.

The French contract Thompsons more than often had serial numbers ranging from 10,000 to 14,000. This example bearing the number 12551 was initially assigned to the GMR (mobile reserve groups) under the Vichy government, then taken by a resistance fighter during a skirmish with a section of the GMR in Savoie.

This photo is an extract from an official assessment report carried out on February 1, 1940, by the technical establishment at Versailles (ETVS) on two 1921 model Thompsons, bearing the serial numbers 10384 and 10171. This preliminary step for the purchase of 3,000 Thompsons by the French Army had the objective of making a choice between the two options proposed by Auto-Ordnance (compensator, type of breech). The first of these two weapons was fitted with a Cutts compensator unlike the second. Both weapons had a breech, an actuator, and a 1928 model recoil system. The French Army finally opted for the basic model, without compensator and with the 1921 model breech and actuator. It is possible that this decision was dictated more by the urgency of the situation than by technical considerations. *CAA*

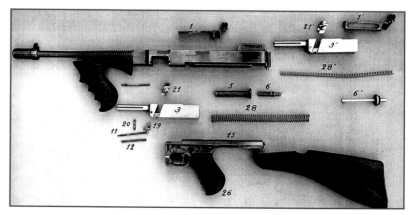

France 1942–44. German parachutist helmet with an MP40 and its magazine, a 1921 Thompson submachine gun with its straight magazines, and the review *Arme Nouvelle* of 1942. *Collection of the Royal Army Museum of Brussels, photo by Marc de Fromont*

L'ARMÉE NOUVELLE

Only the letter "S" preceding the serial number identifies the Thompson made by Savage for Auto-Ordnance.

The maker's initial is found on numerous parts of the weapon; the Blish lock, the breech, the actuator (here the "square" shape of the "S" which resembles a number 5, indicates that it is a part made by the sub-contractor Stevens for Savage), the pitot of the recoil spring, and on the barrel.

Savage rapidly put into production the wood mounted on the Thompson, and also marked it with its initial.

Some 1928 and 1928A1 Thompson models, made by Savage, bear TOMMY GUN on the receiver. It would seem that this was part of an operation destined to register this name to the company.

- The receiver only bore Auto-Ordnance markings, with the exception of all markings identifying the manufacturer as on the Colt made weapons.

The contract finalized between Savage and Auto-Ordnance stated that Savage must not stamp its mark on the weapons apart from the letter "S," preceding the serial number and transferred on the majority of its parts.

The archives of the Savage company, studied by American historian Tracie Hill, however, revealed that 50,000 weapons which were the object of the fourth contract signed between Auto-Ordnance and the manufacturer on November 6, 1940, did not have the prefix "S" before the serial number for a reason still unclear (perhaps it concerned a specific foreign deal?).

Unlike Colt who had the wood for its Thompsons made by Remington, Savage produced its own frames fairly rapidly. Savage had some Thompson parts by

New Manufacturers for the Thompson

Savage Arms Company

Russel Maguire signed a contract for the manufacture of the first batch of 10,000 Thompson 1928 models on December 15, 1939. The Savage Arms Company was at that time a major manufacturer of hunting weapons.

In buying Auto-Ordnance, Russel Maguire also came into possession of manufacturing, equipment, and machine tool plans designed to make the Thompson 1921 model as well as spare parts in stock. In this context, all the necessary conditions came together for Savage to launch the manufacture of the weapon on a large scale.

From April 1940, the factory at Utica, New York, carried out a first delivery of 10,000 Thompson models of 1928, a small number of which were sold by Auto-Ordnance to American police agencies (a variant that American collectors designate as "1928 model commercial") and the majority of which would be purchased later by Great Britain.

It seems that a part of these Savage made model of 1928 Thompsons had been initially destined to satisfy the second French order of 3,000 weapons, but they could not be delivered before the French capitulation of June 1940. This non-delivered batch was probably subsequently sold to Great Britain.

The Savage 1928 models were made with the same tools and sometimes even assembled with the remains of spare parts stock from Colt.

There are only three notable differences:

- The part weighting the bolt handle was not riveted on but machined in one piece.

- The external surfaces were bronzed by the "du-lite" process, which gave them a non-reflective, charcoal grey aspect.

sub-contracting out to its subsidiary "J. Stevens & Company" of Chicopee, Massachusetts. These parts were also marked with an "S" of a slightly more angular profile than the initial "S" that Savage marked on its own productions.

At the same time as producing 1928 model Thompsons both for export and for police forces in the domestic market, Savage also made 1928A1 models for the US Army, whose orders increased during the summer of 1941. From 1941 onwards, Savage ceased to manufacture 1928 models to produce only 1928A1 models.

So as to be able to continue using the old 1928 model marking template until they were definitively worn out, the manufacturer had the markings completed by hand. It can be noted that some Savage made Thompson 1928A1 models bear a serial number lower than 200000 and present the marking US MODEL OF 1928A1 struck over the initials US (not separated by a period) and A1 after the date 1928.

After the serial number 200000, new marking templates permitted the mention "U.S. MODEL OF 1928A1" to be stamped in a regular manner. It can be noted that on these new markings the U and S are followed by a period.

The Thompson submachine gun benefitted from the historical chance of being the only tried and tested submachine gun available on the market in allied countries at the outbreak of the Second World War.

It is highly likely that if the conflict had broken out three or four years later, the Thompson could have been forgotten and that a more modern weapon, with similar features to the British Sten, the German MP38, or the Soviet PPD43 would have seen the light of day.

From February 1941, the Savage factory was in a position to produce 10,000 Thompsons per month. The total production of this site is estimated to have been more than 1.2 million Thompson models 1928, 1928A1, M1, and M1A1. These weapons contributed to the arming of the following:

• British and Commonwealth forces.

• Dutch, Norwegian, and Free French forces.

• Chinese units fighting against Japanese occupation.

They equipped all parts of the US Army and would also be parachuted to resistance fighters in Europe and Asia.

These orders brought considerable profits to the Savage and Auto-Ordnance companies: in 1940, the manufacture of a Thompson cost Savage $32, it was resold to Auto-Ordnance for $67 who invoiced the weapons for $130 each to the US government and $200 to foreign governments. The US treasury considered that Russel Maguire had made improper profits during wartime and claimed a reimbursement of $6 million after the armistice.

Apart from the weapons themselves, it seems that Savage made enough spare parts to assemble 250,000 other weapons. A good proportion of these parts were reused after the war for various remakes of the famous submachine gun.

A Second Production Site at Bridgeport

Maguire predicted that the conflict would last and extended the enterprise to set up his own company through the purchase of an enterprise at Bridgeport, Connecticut, which used to make brake plates. During the first six months of its activity, the factory at Bridgeport only made tools, gauges, and cutting tools. Auto-Ordnance therefore established a stock of tools that came to be extremely precious during the following months when this type of material started to become rare.

The first Thompsons, 1928A1 models made to US Army standards, left Bridgeport in August 1941.

In spite of what Auto-Ordnance wanted people to believe, not all parts of the weapon were made at Bridgeport. However the manufacturer guidelines were so demanding that there was a total interchangeability between the parts made by different suppliers. This explains why it is sometimes possible to come across a barrel stamped with the letter "S" from the Savage factory mounted on a receiver bearing the initial "AO" from the Auto-Ordnance factory.

The Savage Arms Co. made Thompson 1928 models (for Great Britain) along with the majority of 1928A1 models (for Great Britain and the US Army).

The Auto-Ordnance factory at Bridgeport only made 1928A1 models.

After the transfer of the headquarters of Auto-Ordnance to Bridgeport, the markings were modified to make this change apparent.

In total, 5,625,111 Thompson 1928 and 1928A1 models were made from 1940 to 1942 by Savage at Utica, and by Auto-Ordnance in its factory at Bridgeport.

Despite its huge production capacity, the Bridgeport plant never reached maximum production of the 1928A1 model as the US Army adopted a simplified version of this model: the Thompson M1.

From then on the Auto-Ordnance factory of Bridgeport and Savage in Utica converted to the manufacture of the simplified M1 and M1A1 models.

Auto-Ordnance New York marking on a 1921 Thompson. This marking was modified after the company headquarters were transferred to Bridgeport.

Auto-Ordnance Bridgeport marking stamped on the rear of the receiver. This position of the manufacturer's marking is the one most seen on Savage made models (here a 1928 model).

Auto-Ordnance Bridgeport marking stamped in a central position, on the right of the receiver. This position of the manufacturer's marking is the one most seen on 1928A1 models.

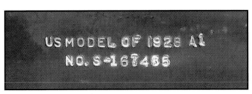

US model of 1928A1 marking obtained by striking by hand "US" and "A1" on a MODEL OF 1928 marking.

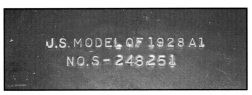

US model of 1928A1 marking stamped in a single go with a new template on a Savage made Thompson with a serial number higher than 200000. Note that the marking is deep, regular, and perfectly aligned.

Marking on a Thompson 1928 model receiver made by Auto-Ordnance of Bridgeport. The initials "AO" in front of the serial number identify the maker. They are repeated on various internal parts of the mechanism as is the letter "S" on weapons made by the Savage Arms Co. The military inspector Waldemar Broberg's initials can be seen. Shown underneath the initials is the new ordnance proof stamp which replaced the flaming bomb: two crossed barrels on a circular belt.

Detail of the marking.

DISASSEMBLY OF THE 1921,

1) Raise magazine catch and slide out magazine.

2) Put the bolt in rearward position and check the absence of cartridge in the chamber.

5) Depress frame latch.

6) Turn safety to "Fire" and pivot to "Full Auto" position. With one hand grasp grip with finger on the trigger as if firing and withdraw frame to rear of gun, pulling down as well as to the rear on frame as it is withdrawn.

8) Slide bolt to the rear.

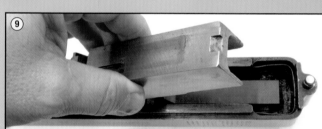

9) Lift out the bolt.

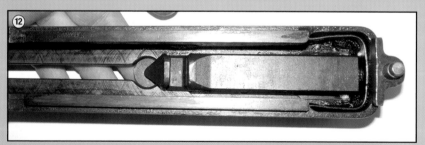

12) Pull the cocking lever back until the arming button is in front of the circular cutout at the top of the case.

13) Remove the cocking lever.

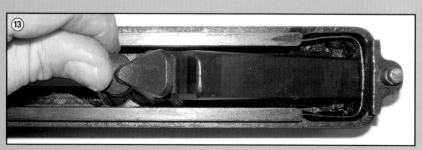

1928, AND 1928 A MODELS

3) For easier handling remove the stock.
Press in on butt stock catch button.

4) Slide butt stock to the rear to remove.

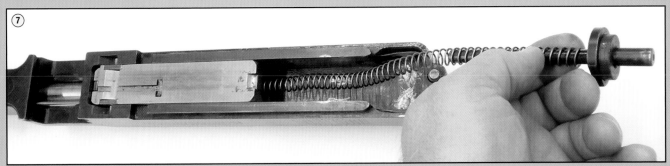

7) Grasp receiver with left hand and with the help of a pin remover press down on buffer pitot then remove it with its recoil spring.

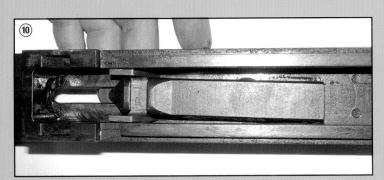

10) Slide actuator with the Blish lock going forward and up.

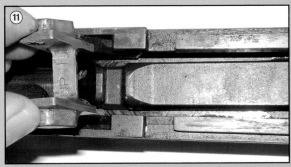

11) Lift out the lock, taking note of the "UP" sign for re-assembly.

Thompson Model 1928 made by Savage, right side.

ASSEMBLY

1) Assembly is made in the reverse order of disassembly. The recoil spring on a Model 1921 Thompson is quite easy to put back in place without a tool because of its wider diameter; it is not the case however with smaller springs used on later models. Therefore it is recommended to use a pin extractor, a nail, or this British tool made specially for assembling the recoil-spring.

2) Insert recoil-spring in the buffer pitot opening, taking care to identify the orifice (arrow).

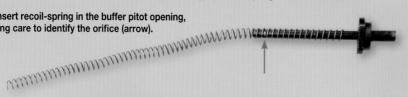

3) Introduce the pin remover in the opening and turn the buffer pitot until the spring is fully compressed. The pin remover should be placed in such a way that removing is easier when in place.

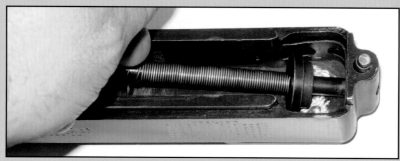

4) Insert buffer pitot and recoil spring.

5) Remove pin remover and release the spring.

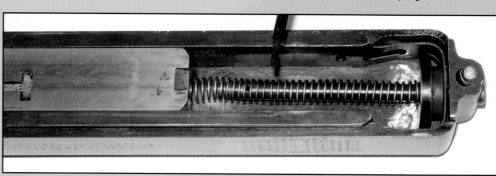

The British Contract 1928 Savage Model

Following the disastrous French campaign in 1939 and 1940, British troops had to leave France as a matter of urgency. The Royal Navy managed to save a maximum number of men from captivity, but the major part of their equipment had to be left behind on the French beaches. In the following months, the United Kingdom found itself threatened with invasion by the German army and with asphyxiation by the cutting off of its supplies by Nazi submarines.

In order to cover this shortage of material the British government dispatched a purchasing mission to the US giving it two primary objectives:

1 to acquire anti-submarine Lockheed Hudson aircraft.

2 to buy as many Thompson submachine guns as possible, along with ammunition, to allow the organization of guerilla type warfare on British soil should the Germans manage to gain a foothold.

The first purchases, made under the principle of "Cash and Carry," rapidly used up the gold reserves the British had in America.

Thompson 1928 model in service in the Scots Guards in 1942. This picture shows clearly the Lee-Enfield slings on the weapons.

The Savage Arms Co. was the main manufacturer of Thompson during the Second World War. It supplied the US Army and its allies with more than 1.2 million Thompson models 1928, 1928A1, and M1A1. *Collection of the Royal Army Museum of Brussels, photo by Marc de Fromont*

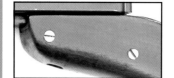

Marking on a Thompson 1928 model bought by Great Britain.

The United States, increasingly aware that the British resistance to the German invasion represented one of the keys to their own security, put into place a procedure to assist their allies: the "Lend-Lease" Act.

This authorized the US government to sell, transfer, exchange, hire, or provide by other means defense equipment to any government where "the President considers the defense is vital to the defense of the United States."

This law, fundamental in the history of the Second World War, was to allow the American armaments industry to supply large numbers of weapons of all types to Great Britain, the Free French forces of North Africa, and the Soviet Union. The value of material supplied from 1941 to 1945 is estimated to be $50 billion.

The British purchasing commission was to order, through successive contracts, a total of around 300,000 Thompson submachine guns from Auto-Ordnance; only a third of those weapons reached Great Britain, the rest ended up at the bottom of the Atlantic, sunk by German U-boats.

These 1928 model Thompsons sometimes bear British reception stamps, or Dutch stamps for those allocated to the Dutch forces.

Transversal screws were fitted by the British to reinforce the butt before the butts with reinforcement braces entered into service.

The "Lend-Lease" crates are unpacked and this British soldier holds a brace of Thompsons. *DR*

The seventh contract signed on March 15, 1941, for the manufacture of 25,000 weapons anticipated the assembly of a flat "1928 Navy" type handguard, with a sling ring instead of the pistol grips previously fitted on the 1928 Savage models. From this contract onwards, the British Thompsons were therefore to be equipped with the same horizontal handguard as on the 1928A1 US Army models.

The start of production of the Sten submachine guns permitted the British to have a weapon made on a large scale for a small price in their own country. They would then stop buying Thompsons from the US.

The Thompsons, already present on British soil, were redistributed to commando units and the outline suggestive of the Thompson 1928 model was integrated into the shoulder badge of the combined operations.

The Thompson 1928, 1928A1, M1, and M1A1 models delivered to the British Army were very frequently modified by transferring the sling rings above the butt and on the left of the handguard and by the installation of transversal reinforcement screws on the first type of butt, lacking a reinforcing crossbolt.

Certain handguards had a crisscrossed, grated surface, this disposition seems to have been mostly applied by the Australian army, whose men operated in the jungle and needed a better grip of the weapon in damp climates.

The French fitted Berthier sling rings on their Thompsons; the British mounted the P.14 sling rings on the forward grip, often on the right side.

British soldier with his Thompson making progress through the Burmese jungle. *DR*

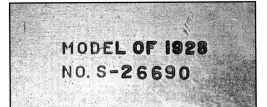

Weapon marking.

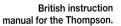

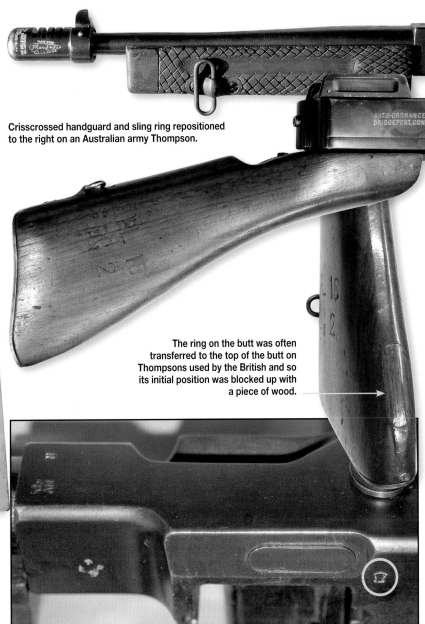

Crisscrossed handguard and sling ring repositioned to the right on an Australian army Thompson.

British instruction manual for the Thompson.

The ring on the butt was often transferred to the top of the butt on Thompsons used by the British and so its initial position was blocked up with a piece of wood.

Reception stamp "W" in a crown on a 1928 British model reassigned to the Dutch free forces.

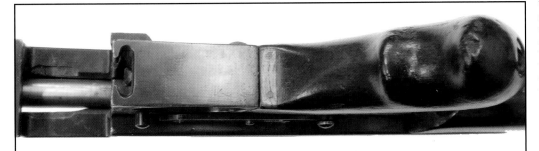

While the American equipment organizations widely practiced the exchange of used parts, the British conscientiously repaired them following traditional armorer techniques, as with the addition of this replacement wooden strip on a damaged pistol grip.

British army 1928 model Thompson. This weapon, bearing the number 26690 is conserved in the collection of the Royal Army Museum in Brussels. A sight bracket has been installed above the chamber. *Collection of the Royal Army Museum of Brussels, Photo VDP*

The first simplification that was brought to the 1928A1 model Thompson during the war was the replacement of the costly Lyman sight by a simple sight bracket.

The sight bracket bore a rudimentary eye piece that was effective for firing up to 100 yards and a sighting notch for firing at 200 yards.

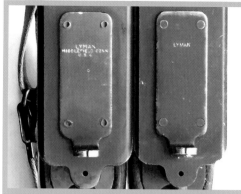

Despite their rudimentary appearance, the brackets are an integral part of sight instruments developed and manufactured by the famous Lyman firm. Two types of markings can be seen here, the one on the left being the most common. On the Thompson in service in the British army the adjustable Lyman sight was often replaced by an unmarked bracket, made in the regimental armories.

War Makes of the 1928A1 Model

From 1940, the American army increased in power in anticipation of a war with Japan in the Pacific or a war against Germany alongside the British. The US Army started to place very large orders of weapons and equipment.

In adopting the Thompson 1928 model, the US Army had demanded that the marking "US ARMY" come before "MODEL OF 1928" and that the marking "A1" be added after so as to take into account the modification of the ejector which was from then on no longer made in a single piece but in two.

Certain specimens of the first deliveries to the US Army were still fitted with a forward vertical pistol grip but the majority of weapons delivered were equipped with a flat handguard, the same profile as on the 1928 US Navy model.

The butt and the handguard were originally equipped with sling rings of the same width as on those of the US 17 so as to allow all types of US Army regulation slings of that period to be fitted.

Originally the weapons destined for the US Army were equipped with a Cutts compensator and an adjustable sight supplied by the Lyman Company.

As the war progressed various simplifications were brought to the machining of certain parts:

- removal of the cooling ribs on the barrel

- replacement of the Lyman sight by a simple bracket in folded steel

- removal of the grid pattern on the bolt handle and safety control handle and the fire mode selector

Bolt handle with grid pattern on a 1928 model Savage Thompson. On this example we can also see a selector with grid pattern, the ejector made in a single piece and the marking "Tommy Gun" where the first letters can be seen at the top of the receiver.

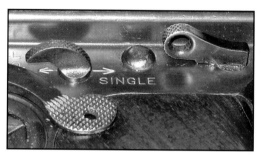

The grid pattern on the safety catch and fire mode selector, along with the perforation on the safety handle identical to that found on the Thompson 1921 model, were abandoned.

Smooth and unperforated safety and selector handle, the former on a late manufacture 1928A1.

- assembly of a compensator without an Auto-Ordnance logo (called type 3 by collectors)

- beechwood replaced walnut for the wooden parts

- reinforcement of the butt grip by a transversal nut and bolt mounted on two steel washers

These were minor improvements which only had a slight bearing on the price of the weapon and the time it took to produce. It has been noted earlier that Auto-Ordnance resold 1928A1 models at an average price of $130 to the US government. This was still a substantial price when it is considered that a Sten Mk.II cost the British government $5 during the same period!

Smooth bolt handle on a late manufacture 1928A1 where the safety and selector handles are smooth and the ejector, as is normal for this model, made in two parts.

British commandos: the 1928 Thompson with drum magazine, beret, two Mills grenades, and a Webley Mk.IV revolver with its canvas case. *Collection of the Royal Army Museum of Brussels, photo by Marc de Fromont*

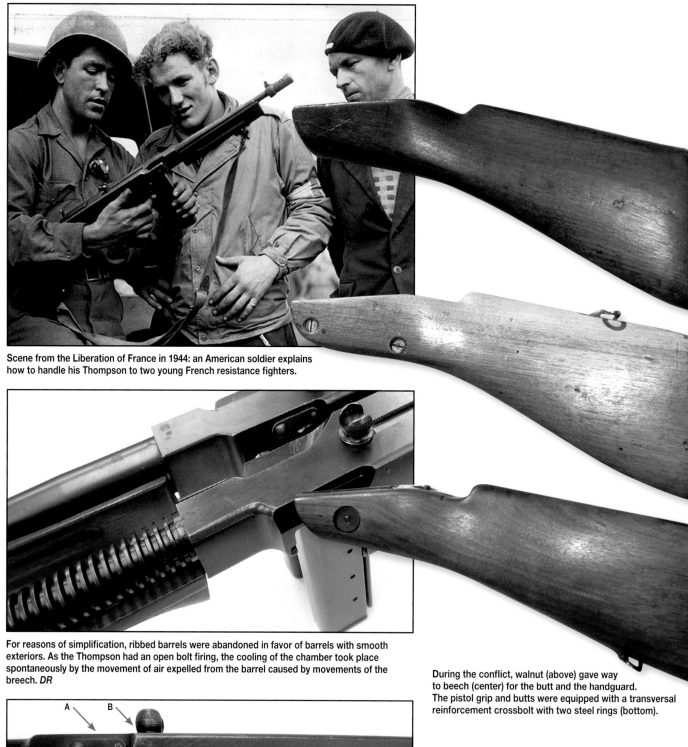

Scene from the Liberation of France in 1944: an American soldier explains how to handle his Thompson to two young French resistance fighters.

For reasons of simplification, ribbed barrels were abandoned in favor of barrels with smooth exteriors. As the Thompson had an open bolt firing, the cooling of the chamber took place spontaneously by the movement of air expelled from the barrel caused by movements of the breech. *DR*

During the conflict, walnut (above) gave way to beech (center) for the butt and the handguard. The pistol grip and butts were equipped with a transversal reinforcement crossbolt with two steel rings (bottom).

The large scale use of the Thompson by the American forces and Allied armies helped to erase the gangsters' weapon image that continued in many minds up until the eve of war. Auto-Ordnance came up with the nickname "Tommy Gun" ("Tommy" being the nickname given to British soldiers). The company registered this name as its own property, and in order to fulfil a clause in US law relative to property rights, Auto-Ordnance was compelled to put the name on some of its weapons. This concerned in general early made 1928A1 models and this name engraved on the top of the receiver gives the weapon an added value for collectors.

Thompson 1928A1 model. The ejector (A) is made in two parts, the actuator knob (B) and the safety and selector catches (C) without grid pattern are proof of the simplifications brought to the machining during wartime.

Thompsons for the USSR

During the last few years collectors have had the great surprise of seeing large amounts of brand new Thompson 1928A1, M1, and M1A1 models arrive from the former USSR.

The large quantity was particularly surprising considering the Thompson had never been a regulation weapon in the USSR.

The origin of these weapons goes back to when large supplies of military vehicles were made by the United States to the USSR in the context of "Lend-Lease." Great quantities of GMC trucks, half-tracks, scout cars, Jeeps, and amphibious vehicles were delivered by sea. The convoys followed the northern route to deliver the equipment to Murmansk and this was extremely hazardous; German aviation, pocket battleships, and U-boats lay in wait for the cargo ships navigating these icy waters. Every ton of equipment delivered to the Red Army was paid for in the blood of the crews that transported it.

The "Lend-Lease" vehicles were delivered complete and in working order with their onboard tools and weaponry in conformity with what had been planned by the US Army. On arrival in the USSR the weapons of a different caliber to Soviet weapons were disembarked and replaced by Soviet equipment. The American weapons thus disembarked were then carefully greased and stocked in the arsenals of the USSR. However, judging by some photos of the period it can be supposed that a small number of them were used for instruction by the Red Army.

Furthermore, it seems that some of these Thompsons fell into the hands of the German forces if we take into account the descriptions identifying the Thompson and the Reising as Russian weapons figuring in identification files of foreign material captured by the *Wehrmacht*. These documents mention the existence of models with a horizontal handguards under the reference "MP 760/2(r)" amongst Russian captured material but also examples with a forward vertical grip (pistol grip) some of which are marked "Model of 1928 (MP 761[r])" and others "Model of 1928 (MP 760[r])." These slight differences indicate that the first Thompsons delivered

The majority of Thompsons on board "Lend-Lease" vehicles sent to the USSR were gathered up and stocked in arsenals to avoid having to ensure the supply of combat units with two different types of submachine gun ammunition. This gives an exceptional character to this photo showing Soviet naval fusiliers armed with 1928A1 model Thompsons. *DR*

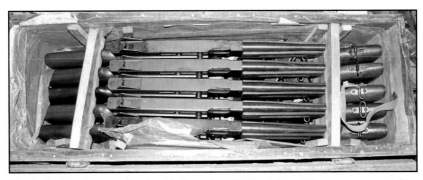

After having been in grease for almost half a century, the "Lend-Lease" Thompsons were resold to Western collectors after the end of the cold war. Here, a case of M1A1 in mint condition after unpacking. *DR*

Between the wars, copies of Thompson model 1921 were made by Chinese arsenals, in caliber 7.63 Mauser and .45 ACP.

to Russia were very certainly Colt made (Model 1921) and early Savage made (Model 1928). This is good news for collectors who can one day hope to see some of these rare versions from arsenals of the ex-Soviet Union come on to the market.

Some were used after the war to keep various "anti-colonialist" rebellions supplied with weapons, at that time unidentifiable. The vast majority of them stayed in their grease, rolled in paper until the end of the cold war. At that time, some wholesalers in surplus material advised that, after neutralizing them, these weapons could be easily sold to Western collectors, especially as they were in a near perfect condition.

Thompsons in China

Around 1930, the Chinese manufactured faithful copies of the 1921 model Thompson in .45 caliber or 7.63 mm Mauser in some state arsenals.

During the Second World War, the Americans abundantly supplied all types of Chinese forces fighting against the Japanese with weapons and ammunition. In this way therefore 1928A1, M1, and M1A1 models got into the hands of Chinese communist and nationalist forces.

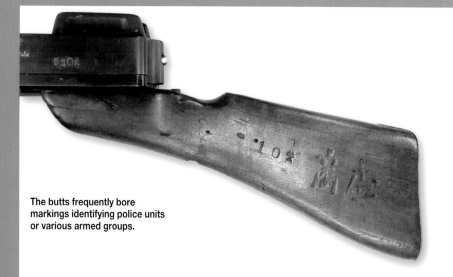

The butts frequently bore markings identifying police units or various armed groups.

The actuator slot, ending in a right angle. We can assume that the model that was the inspiration for this weapon was a particularly early-made 1921 model Thompson.

Comparison between the thickness of the .45 and 7.63 magazines.

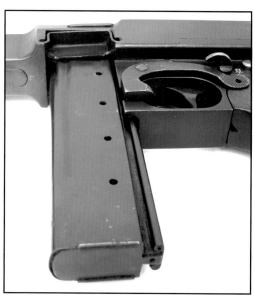

On examples in 7.63 mm caliber it is common for the receiver to be fitted with a dust-protector adapted to the narrower width of the magazine.

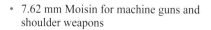

Magazines adapted to the Mauser 7.63 mm cartridge dimensions (right) were ordered from the United States by China. They generally bear the markings of Auto-Ordnance or those of the firm SW Co. On the left a standard .45 ACP 20-round cartridge for comparison.

Fire selector and safety catch markings.

After the Japanese defeat, the struggle for power began between communists and nationalists and resulted in victory for the communist forces in 1949.

Once in power, the communists benefitted from the support of the USSR for several years, which led them to standardize their weaponry based on the ammunition supplied by their allies:

- 7.62 mm Moisin for machine guns and shoulder weapons

- 7.62 mm Tokarev for submachine guns and hand weapons.

As numerous Thompsons were available in the territory controlled by the communists, it was decided to convert them to 7.62 mm Tokarev. To do this, the barrel was replaced by a 7.62 mm tube, often recut in a Moisin or Maxim 1910 barrel. The magazine housing was widened and fitted with an adaptor for a magazine for 7.62 mm caliber cartridges. Two grooves were cut into the lower part of the breech to enable it to pass over the magazine lips.

Many of these weapons were subsequently transferred to the North Korean then North Vietnamese forces. The latter did not hesitate to transform the Thompson, retrieved from the French expeditionary corps in the Far East and American and South Vietnamese forces, into 7.62 mm Tokarev caliber.

The transformation which uses an adaptor allowing the weapon to be fed with the help of a curved Sudarev submachine gun magazine seems to be the most successful one.

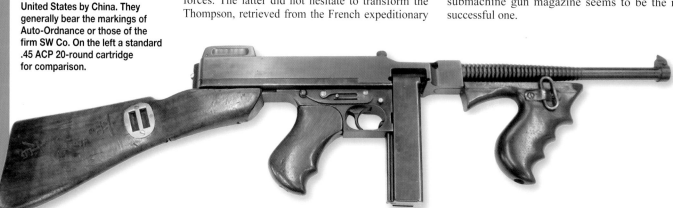

A sling loop based on those on the PPSh 41 Soviet submachine gun.

The Thompson M1 and M1A1

In the chapter devoted to model 1928A1 war productions we have mentioned the simplifications that intervened in its manufacture.

In December 1941, when the Japanese attack on Pearl Harbor was about to bring the United States into war, John Pearce, an engineer of British origin employed by Savage since 1920, and Nicholas L. Brewer, a designer in the Stevens factory closely associated with Savage, suggested the removal of the Blish lock on the Thompson 1928 model.

This part had its use on weapons firing very high pressure rounds but revealed itself to be superfluous on Thompsons firing a .45 automatic pistol cartridge. The use of this lock imposed an internal machining of the receiver of the weapon in order to carry out the unlocking slides on the Blish lock. It represented a waste of time and money.

A new Thompson without breech locking was adopted by the US Army on March 24, 1942 (therefore very rapidly), under the name "Submachine gun cal.45 M1."

Compared with the 1928A1 model it presented the following simplifications:

- Removal of the Blish lock and the lubrication system of the breech.

- Permanent abandonment of feeding by drum magazine. The magazine well of the Thompson M1 was only machined to receive straight magazines and the lateral slot for positioning the drum magazine was removed. On the other hand a 30-round magazine was brought into service to conserve an equivalent capacity to most other submachine guns.

- Removal of the Cutts compensator which was simply removed on the model M1.

- Barrel devoid of cooling flanges.

- Simplified machining of the handguard support.

- "L"-shaped sight pierced with an eyepiece for firing up to 100 yards and a sighting notch cut at the top for firing up to 200 yards.

- Narrower receiver than on the 1928A1 model and fitted with a lateral bolt handle.

- Butt screwed on the frame.

- Simplified selector and safety handle.

On this early made Thompson M1 (number 25232) the selector and safety handles are of the type previously used on 1928A1 models.

Markings on an M1 bearing the serial number 262265. It is fitted with an "L"-shaped rear sight.

THOMPSON SUBMACHINE GUN
CALIBER .45 M1
NO 72661

Detail of the weapon markings. On the M1, the marking identifying the manufacturer is no longer in front of the serial number but under the receiver at the level of the chamber Also, the term "caliber" replaces "calibre," used on 1921 and 1928A1 models.

On these M1 and M1A1, the manufacturer's mark ("S" for Savage, as seen here, or "AOC" for Auto-Ordnance corporation) no longer appears, as on the 1928 and 1928A1 models, in front of the serial number but under the chamber.

Second version of the Thompson M1 fitted with the second model of a protected rear sight.

GEG marking in a circle. George E. Goll was delegated by Auto-Ordnance to carry out inspections of Thompsons at the Savage factory prior to presentation to the military inspector. The initials "FJA" (Lt. Col. Frank J. Atwood) appeared under the "GEG" stamp and under the ordnance mark (two crossed barrels on a circle representing a belt).

On the M1 the receiver serial number is transferred under the trigger guard.

"S" for Savage hallmark on the barrel of an M1A1.

"AOC" hallmark on the barrel of an M1A1 made by the Auto-Ordnance Corporation.

Angular "S" hallmark (resembling a number 5) on a foresight delivered by Stevens to the Savage factory.

After several months, the "L"-shaped rear sight proved an obstruction: it had the tendency to get caught up in equipment and clothing. It was replaced by an "L"-shaped rear sight but equipped with two lateral protections. This modification appeared on the Thompson M1 with a serial number higher than 137000.

In October 1942, a final modification was decided: the non-fixed firing pin actioned by a triangle that knocks against the rear section of the chamber when the breech closes was replaced by a fixed firing pin and the breech became a single firing mass. From that moment, the breech which previously was simply polished from then on had a bronze finish. This new version of the Thompson was called the M1A1.

The Thompson M1A1 began manufacture from the end of 1942 at both Savage and Auto-Ordnance. The numbering of the M1A1 started at No. 850000.

The price invoiced to the US government was around $36 per M1A1 (the price of seven Stens!).

Some Thompson M1s were fitted with a fixed bolt with firing pin in the arsenal. In this case the mention A1 was generally stamped by hand after the marking, "THOMPSON SUBMACHINE GUN M1."

Features of the Thompson M1 and M1A1	
Caliber	.45 (11.43 mm)
Ammunition	45 ACP
Total length	81.5 cm
Barrel length	26.7 cm
Weight without magazine	4.75 kg
Weight with 20-round magazine	5.32 kg
Weight with 30-round magazine	5.48 kg

This weapon is fitted with simplified safety and selector handles mounted in a standard way on the M1 and M1A1.

Comparison between an M1 breech still equipped with an independent cam-actioned firing pin, as on 1921 and 1928 models, and that of a M1A1 with fixed firing pin on which the cam has been removed.

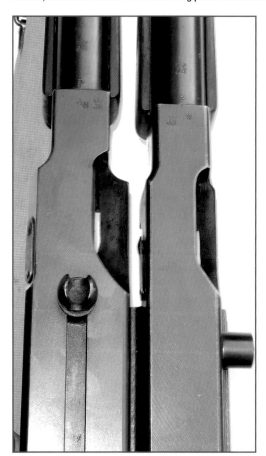

Comparison between a receiver on a Thompson model 1928A1 (left) and the narrower M1 (right).

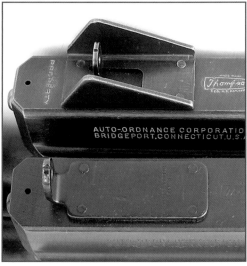

Comparison between two types of sight.

Marking on the left side of the receiver on an M1.

The Thompson M1 and M1A1 remained in service in the French Army until the end of the Algerian war in 1962. *Collection of the Royal Army Museum of Brussels, photo by Marc de Fromont*

DISASSEMBLY OF THE M1

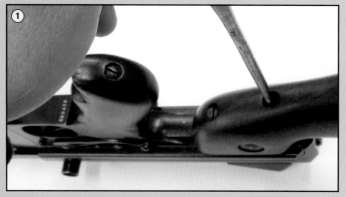

1) Raise magazine catch and slide out magazine. Put the bolt in rearward position and check the absence of cartridge in the chamber. Unscrew the two butt stock screws. It is not necessary to remove the butt stock group to remove frame.

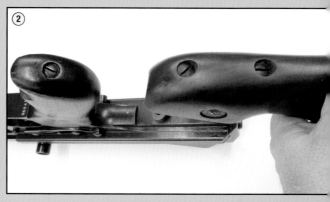

2) Remove the stock.

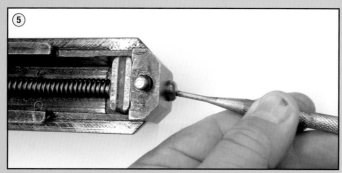

5) Grasp receiver with left hand and with the help of a pin remover press down on buffer pitot.

6) Do not release the pressure on the pitot. Press the buffer pitot slightly into the receiver and withdraw the buffer.

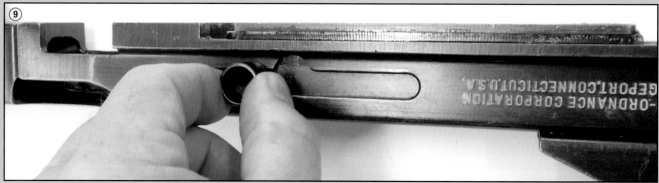

9) Slide the bolt rearward and tip the rear end until the bolt handle rests in the semicircular cut on the right side of the receiver. Steady the bolt in this position. Press the bottom of the hammer rearward to disengage the bolt handle.

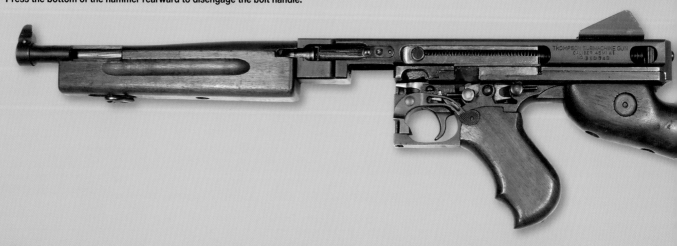

AND M1A1

3) Compress frame latch.

4) See that safety is at FIRE and rocker pivot is at FULL AUTO. Grasp the bolt handle in the retracted position with one hand and with the other squeeze the trigger, allowing the bolt to move slowly forward on an empty chamber. Take gun from knee or table, grasping receiver with left hand, squeeze the trigger and slide the frame off to the rear.

7) The shock absorber buffer, made of compressed rubber to absorb vibrations, is held within two steel plates.

8) Gradually pull out the pitot with recoil spring.

10) Remove the handle.

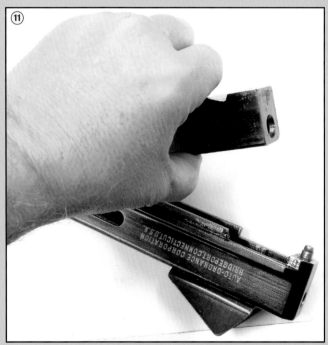

11) Remove the bolt from the receiver.

MAGAZINES

As the Thompson submachine gun was intended to be used as a support weapon its designers gave their attention to a high capacity magazine.

This was how the drum magazine "C," with a capacity for 100 cartridges, came into being. A .45 ACP cartridge weighing a little more than twenty-one grams, we can easily deduce the considerable extra weight of the weapon. Its manufacture was soon therefore abandoned and the majority of examples produced ended up in Ireland along with several illicit 1921 model Thompsons.

For missions which did not necessitate such firepower, the weapon could be fed by straight 20-round magazines (XX). Auto-Ordnance replaced this accessory with a 50-round magazine, type "L," not as heavy, less cumbersome, and less likely to jam.

Manufacturers

The manufacturers of diverse types destined for the Thompson were made by various American subcontractors.

The "L" magazines made before 1940 bore the address of Auto-Ordnance New York. Those destined for the Thompson 1921 model received a marking mentioning that the key placed at the forward of the magazine must be wound to eleven clicks, in order to put the correct tension on the recoil spring. On the magazines destined for the Thompson 1928 model, it is mentioned that the key must be wound to nine clicks.

During the Second World War the "L" magazines made for Auto-Ordnance received the new company address at Bridgeport.

Several subcontractors made "L" magazines for the US Army and its allies:

- Seymour Products Company

- Crosby Company of Buffalo, New York (marking "The Crosby Co" or C co)

- Charles Fischer Spring Company. This company, having been supplied with out-of-date plans by the US government meant the magazines were defective and had to be destroyed.

- Worcester Pressed Steel Company (marking: WPS or WPS Co)

Unlike straight magazines which were fitted from under the magazine housing with breech closed or open, the drum magazines slid laterally in the weapon and could not be put into place if the breech was in a rear position.

The magazine follower on straight magazines has a finger guard which blocks the breech in a rear position after the firing of the last round, whereas the drum magazines do not have a finger guard.

Twenty-round Thompson magazines. It can be seen here the marking of five different manufacturers. The two magazines on the left bear variations of the Auto-Ordnance markings.

From left to right: 30-round magazine with magazine viewing holes closed up by aluminum rivets, to stop sand from getting inside during amphibious operations. Standard 30-round magazine with a beautiful original blue-black finish. Thirty-round magazine phosphate coated during reconditioning.

Twenty-shot magazines were also made by various companies and most of them were also engaged in the manufacture of the "L" magazine.

- Auto-Ordnance who in reality did not make magazines, but stamped its mark on magazines supplied by subcontractors.

- Seymour Products Company

- Spark-Withington Company (marking SW co)

- Worcester Pressed Steel Company (marking WPS)

- Crosby Company

Furthermore, some marginal productions are a cause of great joy for the collector today; for example the straight 18-round magazines adapted to "multiple slug" .45 Peters cartridges, and the magazines dimensioned for .351 SL cartridges that were fired by some prototypes, or the mysterious 20-round 7.63 caliber Mauser magazines made for China by Auto-Ordnance and Spark-Withington Company.

Adoption of the Straight Magazine

When the technicians at the Auto-Ordnance factory proposed a reshaped Thompson with a faster and more economical manufacture (which was to become the Thompson M1) to the US Army, it was decided to abandon the drum magazine. The Thompson M1 was to be machined without the lateral guideway which allowed the drum magazine to be slid laterally to its locking position on the 1921, 1928, and 1928A1 models. As compensation, a straight magazine with a greater capacity (30 rounds) was adopted. This version was made by factories which previously had produced 20-round cartridges.

As for the 50-round drum magazines, they were declared obsolete on November 29, 1944, and the order was given to destroy those in stock with the exception of 50,000 specimens which were stored in a depot in South Dakota.

The Numrich Arms Company relaunched the manufacture of Thompson after the Second World War and this company took into account the very high demand from collectors for the drum magazine to be marketed once again. Numrich therefore had made a magazine of this type containing only forty rounds and marked with the address "West Hurley – New York." When Auto-Ordnance took over Numrich Arms, it once again produced 50-round drum magazines as well as an identical replica of the C 50-round magazine. Following the sales limits placed on high-capacity magazines, Auto-Ordnance marketed a drum magazine externally identical to the L model but containing only ten cartridges.

Twenty-round magazine bearing a stenciled French Army stock number.

Various manufacturers' markings on 30-round cartridges.

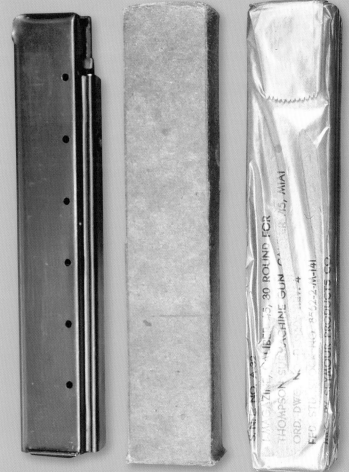

Once they were wrapped in oiled paper, the magazines were then placed in cardboard which protected them from impact during transport.

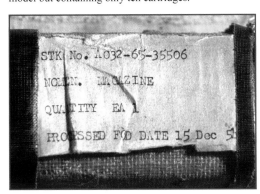

Stock label fixed on tulle wrapping on a 30-round magazine after transit to the arsenal for reconditioning.

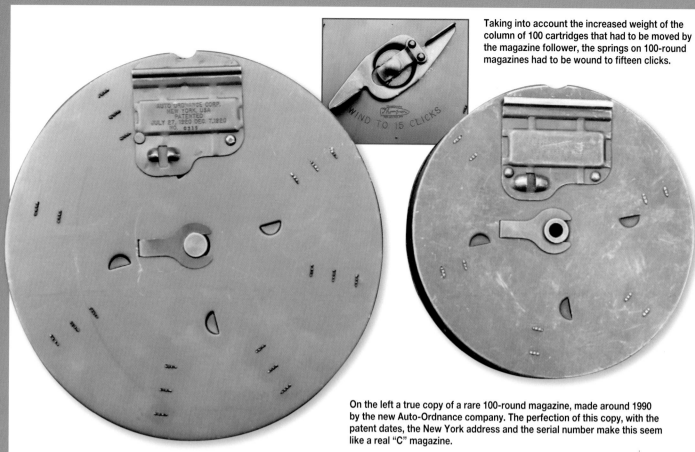

Taking into account the increased weight of the column of 100 cartridges that had to be moved by the magazine follower, the springs on 100-round magazines had to be wound to fifteen clicks.

On the left a true copy of a rare 100-round magazine, made around 1990 by the new Auto-Ordnance company. The perfection of this copy, with the patent dates, the New York address and the serial number make this seem like a real "C" magazine.

Famous photo of a soldier filling the magazines by candlelight and without much enthusiasm the day before a firing exercise. The soldier is wearing a uniform from the beginning of the war, very similar to the First World War battledress, and a flat 1917 model helmet. *DR*

Marking on a 50-shot drum magazine made in the twenties and bearing the address of Auto-Ordnance in New York.

The New York address of the company fixed on the other side of the magazine. The magazines made by Savage during the Second World War would be marked Auto-Ordnance Bridgeport.

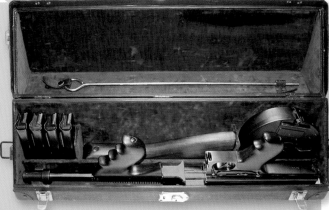

A rigid transport box (in reality a faithful reproduction of the 1920s model, the internal layout is the "FBI type")
where the weight of the 50-round magazine is balanced out by that of the four 20-round magazines and the disassembled butt is placed in the middle.
A cleaning rod and cleaning kit are fixed under the lid.

A British wooden box to transport a Thompson 1928A1 model and its accessories. Even though it is smaller, this box is based on those which were intended for the transport of Vickers machine guns and Bren and Lewis light machine guns. *DR*

A protective cover for onboard weapons in open vehicles (jeep, motorcycle, half-track, etc.).

British breech protector in canvas.

Thompson 1928A1 model in its cover positioned in the leather saddle holster of a Harley-Davidson motorcycle. Of course the weapon was removed from its cover in danger zones.

Various types of wooden cases were organized in a small-scale way to allow the discrete transport of a Thompson and its magazines.

Transport cover for a Thompson butt, a cleaning rod (placed in an inside pocket), and four 20-shot magazines. This cover could be transported on the shoulder, as a holster, or attached to the saddle of a horse.

Magazine carrier for a 50-round drum.

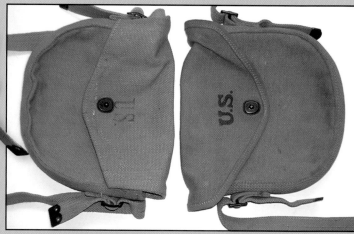

Comparison between the American and British version of the drum magazine carrier.

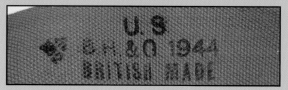

Marking on the suspension sling.

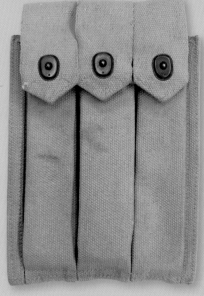

When the 30-round magazine was adopted, the US Army put into service this model of magazine carrier for three 30-round magazines.

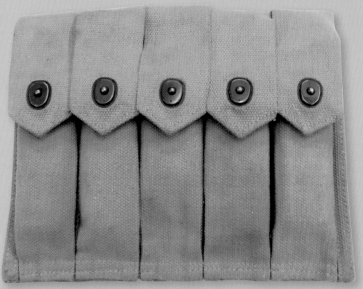

The Mills company specialized in making canvas military equipment and made, during the twenties, magazine carriers with four compartments, for 20-shot magazines, for the Auto-Ordnance company. When the US Army adopted the Thompson 1928A1 model, the same type of magazine carriers were made but for the transport of five magazines (100 cartridges).

This type of magazine carrier in a more supple canvas was put at the disposal of men equipped with Thompsons a little after the United States entered the war in 1942. It appears on many photos of combats in Normandy.

The back of a supple magazine carrier. Like all American equipment of both wars, this type of magazine carrier that was found for a low price in surplus stores of the seventies has become very rare over time. This equipment is now much copied in Asia and it is often difficult to tell the difference between the reproductions and the real thing as the markings are so faithful to the originals.

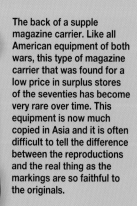

Marking of the manufacturer Rusco.

SLINGS. AND ACCESSORIES

Kerr type sling, made by the "Kerr adjustable strap company," was adopted in 1917 for Springfield 1903 and US 17 rifles. A slightly shorter version was put into service under the name "M3 sling" for the Thompson. We can see here the standard model in light khaki with brass buckles bearing the name "Nobucki." There were later variations in olive green canvas and with steel, phosphate-coated buckles.

Original wrapping of a Kerr sling reconditioned by the Naval equipment depot in Norfolk.

1923 model sling mounted on a US 17 rifle.

Steel parkerised buckle from a late manufactured olive green canvas Kerr sling.

Generally, all the slings conceived for American rifles could be mounted on the Thompson. SSgt. Cyril V. Krotzer, photographed in April 1944, carries his Thompson M1A1 with a 1923 model sling easily identifiable by its buckle which is slightly in front of the Mk.II grenade fixed to his belt suspenders. *US National Archives*

American soldier at war. Note the magazine holder with five compartments with flaps positioned at an angle so as to prevent the magazines from falling out at the same time as allowing their quick access. *DR*

Three oil cans: from left, in nickeled brass is for the Thompson 1921 model. The one in the center in polished brass and right covered in cracked black paint are both for 1928 and 1928A1 models.

Marking on an oil can in polished brass. The majority of Thompson oil cans have no markings.

Variations of cleaning rods in brass, in steel with a brass tip, and steel only. The bronze and horsehair chamber brushes, contained in the model 1912 Colt 1911A1 maintenance boxes, was screwed on to the end of these rods. They can thus be fitted with a flannelette pull-through.

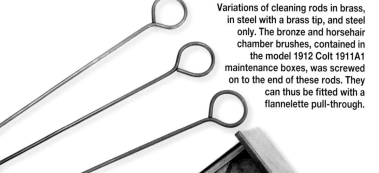

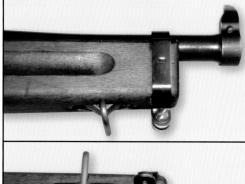

Handguard brace which started to appear at the end of the Second World War to prevent cracking.

American soldier watching over a group of German prisoners. His M1A1 Thompson is fitted with a handguard brace. The sling appears to be in M1 canvas from a Garand rifle. *DR*

Tool of British origin used for winding the recoil spring on 1928 and 28 A1 Thompsons.

Chamber brush for .45 caliber submachine gun, made in 1943 and still bearing the maker's label "the Fuller Brush Co."

Spare breech for Thompson M1A1 in its storage wrapping.

Thompson with silencer: this model seems to have been developed after the war for the US Special Forces and their allies. They could still be seen in the hands of the COMSUBIN (Italian marine commandos) around 1980.

CHAPTER 4

THE THOMPSON AFTER THE SECOND WORLD WAR

Conversion from a Thompson American model 1928A1 to a 7.62 mm Tokarev. The barrel was replaced by a 7.62 mm barrel; the magazine is a PM Sudarev PPS 43 that an ingenious adapter has kept in the weapon, the breech is filed with two guideways in its lower part to avoid blocking on the lips of the 7.62 mm magazine which are more narrowly spaced than on those of .45 ACP magazines.

A merican submachine guns of the Second World War were used for a long time after the end of the conflict and, with the exception of the M3 and M3A1, the majority were of old design. They used a .45 ACP cartridge, far less common than the 9 mm Parabellum used by NATO armies, and 7.62 Tokarev in service in communist armies. This persistence is explained by the enormous quantities of weapons made by American industry during the war and by the fact that the US had an abundant distribution of their war surplus in the context of various programs of military aid with their allies:

- 15,000 Thompsons model 1921 and 1928 were made by Colt in 1921 and 1922.

- 1,750,000 1928, 1928A1, M1 ,and M1A1 models were produced between 1939 and 1944. Of this number 1,250,000 were made by Savage, which ensured the manufacture of the vast majority of the 1928A1.

After refusing to equip itself with different submachine guns proposed to them by various private inventors, including the Hyde M2 submachine gun, the American Army adopted a new submachine gun more in accordance with modern manufacturing techniques, which was christened the M3. The manufacture of the Thompson was stopped in 1944.

New Makes

After the Second World War, more or less faithful copies of the Thompson were made in a restricted number in Vietnam, Turkey, and Egypt.

In February 1944, foreseeing the end of the war, Russel Maguire stopped the manufacture of Thompsons at Auto-Ordnance and began to convert his enterprise in order to make consumer goods.

All the equipment necessary for the manufacture of the Thompson, along with spare parts and the rights related to this activity were given to a toy manufacturer "Kilgore Manufacturing Company," which planned to resell the equipment to the Egyptian government.

When this project failed, in 1949, Kilgore resold everything connected with the manufacture of Thompson to the Numrich Company of West Hurley, New York, without even making an inventory of the stock that Auto-Ordnance had given it.

Groove machined on the lower side of the breech. Zones that have been soldered can be seen, corresponding probably to repairs made to a damaged part.

The ingenious adaptor for a Sudarev magazine, which slides in place of the 45 ACP magazine.

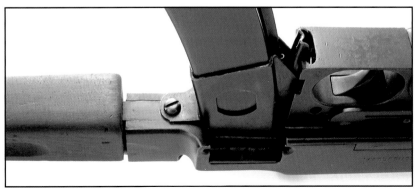

The adaptor is maintained by a simple screw at the front and by a stud at the rear which slides in the T-shaped groove normally designed for the .45 magazine. The .45 magazine catch, unnecessary in this configuration, has been removed.

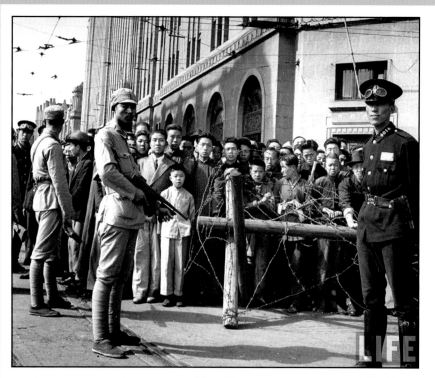

Thompson 1921 model used for keeping order by the Chinese Army in Shanghai in 1945. *DR*

Numrich selected several particularly interesting receivers, bearing 1921 and 1928 Navy markings, that it completed with parts drawn from Auto-Ordnance stocks and these weapons were then sold to collectors.

A New Passion

The arrival of these weapons on the market, at the same time as the publication of William J. Helmer's book *The Gun That Made the Twenties Roar*, triggered a passion for the history of the Thompson and the collection of the weapon and its accessories in the United States.

The first book on the Thompson was written by Frederick Willis, who was for a time the vice president of Auto-Ordnance. He self-published a work entitled *Tommy*, (referring to the nickname "Tommy Gun" given to the weapon). This canvas bound book bore a reduced metal model of a Thompson under perspex on its cover. Willis' work meant the essential details of the Thompson were conserved and its facts were incorporated and developed in Helmer's work. The in-depth exploration was continued by Tracie L. Hill, president of the "Thompson Collector's Association," who collected information gathered by its members, and synthesized it with information obtained by her own research to form a monumental work: *Thompson, the American Legend*, published in 1996; and *Thompson, the Ultimate Book*, published in 2009.

Thompson submachine guns today have real cult status in the United States, where amateurs can collect them in firing condition by having a Class III license. Exhibit versions are made of authentic parts mounted on receivers molded in alloys, and appear identical to authentic models. Unlike France, it is the receivers and frames which are classed in the US, whereas the barrels, breeches, and other parts are available over-the-counter.

Numrich was a company that specialized in the sale of spare parts of weapons and bought stocks from firms that had disappeared in order to replenish its funds.

When opening the crates bought from Kilgore, the staff was surprised to find, apart from a huge quantity of spare parts, near-complete weapons, rare prototypes such as the Thompson BSA, Thompson 1919 model, versions in caliber .30 M1, and even a rare automatic Blish pistol.

For the Shooters

Shooters could also get ahold of semi-automatic versions of weapons made by Auto-Ordnance that had been bought by a former employee of Numrich, Ira Trast, who was convinced that a semi-automatic version of the Thompson, destined for shooters of historic weapons, could be manufactured again. In 1974, he contacted the BATF (Bureau for Alcohol, Tobacco, Firearms, and Explosives: the Federal Service that has control over the rating of weapons in the USA) to put their expertise to the test concerning two semi-automatic prototypes fitted with a 40 cm barrel and without fire selector, christened "model of 1927."

These prototypes were not certified for commercial sale by the BATF which considered with justification that their retro-conversion to continuous burst fire weapons was too easy and therefore contravened the provisions of the 1968 "Gun Control Act" prohibiting unlisted automatic weapons.

Giving a Thompson M1A1 to a "*harki*" (Muslim Algerians who served as auxiliaries in the French Army). The abandonment of these partisans, after the Evian Accord of 1962, that the French Army had pushed to engage against the rebellion is without doubt a reason for guilt and "repentance" in this somber period in French history. *DR*

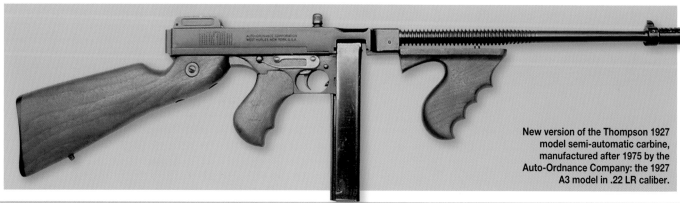

New version of the Thompson 1927 model semi-automatic carbine, manufactured after 1975 by the Auto-Ordnance Company: the 1927 A3 model in .22 LR caliber.

Thompson during the Pacific War. *Collection of the Royal Army Museum of Brussels, photo by Marc de Fromont*

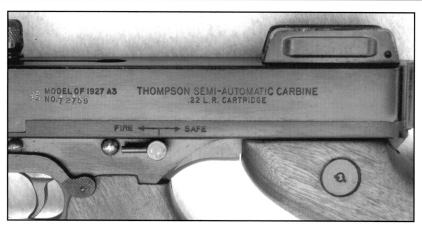

Marking on a Thompson semi-automatic carbine 1927 A3 model. The proof stamp AR made by the Saint Etienne test facility when the weapon was imported in France is visible. (The purchase and ownership of .22 LR caliber semi-automatic carbines was possible in France until 1995).

Changing of the gangway guard on board a Taiwanese navy gun-boat. *DR*

The 1927 A3 model carbine was fed by a 10-round magazine concealed in the body of an authentic Seymour magazine conceived for 30 .45 caliber cartridges. A curved magazine exists for this weapon and a dummy drum containing a magazine for 10 .22 LR cartridges.

In 1975, a version of the 1927 model Thompson carbine, modified to prevent any conversion to automatic fire, was finally authorized by the BATF. Once the green light had been received, the commercialization of the new Auto-Ordnance Thompsons could be launched. Several of these weapons arrived in France where they were owned by marksmen holding a Class B gun license. A version of the 1927 model carbine, called 1927 A3 caliber .22 LR, was marketed in France in the eighties but the grading of the .22 LR semi-automatic carbines in the fourth category from 1995 in France brought the sale of this weapon to a halt.

Some Thompsons, having kept the continuous burst fire feature, were made in the USA for collectors that held a Class III license, as well as for American police units and a final military contract was concluded just before the invasion of Kuwait for the personal guard of the Emir.

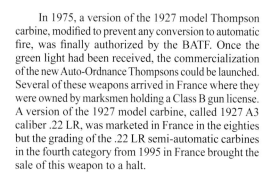

This 1921 model Thompson has been reassembled from authentic parts found in crates bought from Kilgore by the Numrich Arms Company. The beech frame moved away from the American brown-red walnut that was a feature on the original Colt 1921 and 1922 models. American collectors nonetheless snapped them up when they appeared on the market. *Champlin Museum, photo by Alan Gruening*

CHAPTER 5

THE M3 SUBMACHINE GUN: "GREASE GUN"

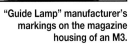

The M3, recognizable by its bolt handle reminiscent of a crank handle.

"Guide Lamp" manufacturer's markings on the magazine housing of an M3.

A group of American Coast Guard reservists with an Oerlikon 20 mm gun at firing practice. One of the men positioned at the rear carries an M3 submachine gun across his chest.

Presentation

The outline of the weapon is reminiscent of that of the German MP40. Its solid appearance led to it being called "Grease Gun" by American soldiers.

The M3 submachine gun consists of five main parts:

- the cylindrical-shaped receiver which continues to the base of a pistol grip at the rear and a magazine housing at the front. This is composed of two half cylinders pressed then welded. The gun sights are made up of an eyesight made by pressing and a foresight borne on the forward part of the receiver, a clamping spring riveted on the left of the receiver retains a cylindrical oil can, which is none other than that of the USM1 carbine. Two metal trigger guards, welded on the left side of the receiver.

F rom the beginning of 1941, the US Army ordnance undertook to develop a weapon inspired by the most modern submachine guns of the period: the German MP40 and the British Sten.

The future submachine gun of the American Army had to be a short, compact weapon with a retractable butt and made entirely of metal, essentially from standard quality, shaped, and welded steel sheets.

The general contractor of this project was Col. René Studler of the ordnance, who was assisted by the inventor George Hyde, along with an engineer from General Motors, Frederick Sampson.

This team rapidly reached the stage of a prototype equipped with selective fire capacity called "T15." The rate of fire of the weapon was judged sufficiently slow to allow the exemption of a fire selector. This was removed and a new version with only automatic fire capabilities, called "T20," continued the tests. Five T20 prototypes were tested with success in November 1942 at the Aberdeen shooting ranges. The positive result was confirmed by tests in regiments carried out during amphibious operations, by among others the Armored Corps, who came to the conclusion that the new weapon was excellent and its accuracy and imperviousness to foreign bodies proved to be superior to those of other submachine guns in service. The official adoption of the "T20" under the name of "Submachine gun caliber .45 M3" was announced on December 24, 1942.

The manufacture of the weapon was ensured by a subsidiary of General Motors specialized in stamped steel pieces: the Guide Lamp Company. The manufacture of some barrels was subcontracted out to Marlin Firearms, and some barrel bases to Buffalo Arms.

The ejection port cover has a lug on its internal side which engages in an orifice on the breech and stops accidental recoil. This cover must be opened by hand before arming the weapon.

Close up of the bolt handle.

Left side view of a US M3. In the middle of the frame the M1 carbine oiler housing is visible (absent on the photo).

Oiler in position.

Rubber caps to cover the lips of the exposed magazines were put into service at the end of the war. One of these caps can be seen here placed on an M3 magazine next to the tool to load the magazines, which gave inspiration to the postwar French MAT 49 submachine gun.

Allowing a sling to be fixed (also that of a US carbine). A rectangular shaped ejection port cover ensures its imperviousness; this part, slightly curved to correspond to the shape of the receiver, bears a lining on its internal side to reinforce imperviousness when the cover is closed. On this internal side, there is also a hook-shaped steel piece held by two rivets. When the cover is closed and the breech is forward, this part engages in a cavity in the breech and prevents it from moving backwards. If the breech is at the back and the cover is closed, this part blocks the path of the breech in case it becomes loose and prevents it from chambering and striking a cartridge. This rudimentary system was nonetheless effective and was the only safety system on the weapon.

- The mobile breech, a single striking mass, sliding on two parallel rods, surrounded by the recoil springs.

- The lower block, on which a bolt handle, in crank handle form, is mounted.

- The barrel, a single 20-cm long cylindrical tube, bearing four grooves is mounted and pinned on a disc-shaped base with threads at the rear so it can be screwed into the receiver. The rim of this part is serrated and a spring positioned under the receiver prevents it from unscrewing accidentally.

- The butt, single, folded steel rod, slides in the guideway positioned on either side of the receiver. A catch placed at the rear of the receiver can be screwed in three positions.

Laid out in this way, the weapon is particularly interesting for arming both parachutists and vehicles. The M3 submachine gun and its successor: the M3A1 was to be the onboard weapon on American armored vehicles until the dawn of the year 2000.

Use

The weapon is heavy but not as heavy as a Thompson, above all it is easy to handle and very well balanced.

Its weak point is the bolt handle which when used proved to be quite fragile. The replacement of the block bearing the bolt handle is easy but not possible during

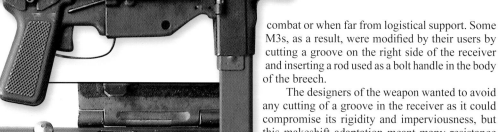

The bolt handle of the M3 was frequently out of order, some parachutist units removed it and simply replaced it with an arming rod pushed in the breech and slid into a groove machined in the receiver.

Detail of a modified bolt handle.

combat or when far from logistical support. Some M3s, as a result, were modified by their users by cutting a groove on the right side of the receiver and inserting a rod used as a bolt handle in the body of the breech.

The designers of the weapon wanted to avoid any cutting of a groove in the receiver as it could compromise its rigidity and imperviousness, but this makeshift adaptation meant many resistance fighters could continue using their M3 weapons in the absence of spare parts. It seems that some commandos carried out this modification before leaving on a mission.

During use, it was also noted that the magazine release catch was subject to impacts, which could cause an accidental unscrewing of the magazine, which, considering the weight of an M3 magazine loaded with .45 cartridges meant that fails of this part were inevitable.

Last American submachine gun adopted during the Second World War, the M3 and its simplified version: the M3A1, were to be used up until the Vietnam War by the American infantry and would remain in service on armored vehicles up until the 1980s. *Collection of the Royal Army Museum of Brussels, photo by Marc de Fromont*

AUGUST 14, 1950
INTERNATIONAL EDITION

24TH DIVISION
SOLDIERS AT FRONT

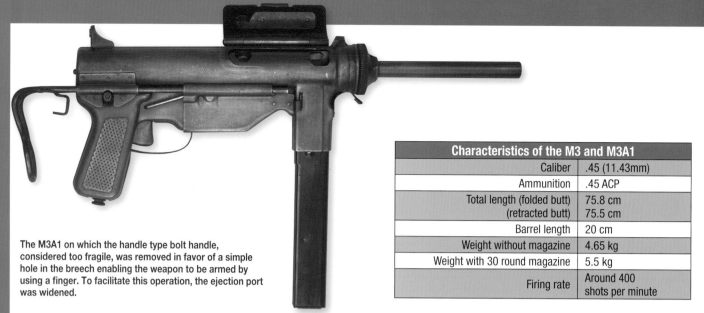

Characteristics of the M3 and M3A1	
Caliber	.45 (11.43mm)
Ammunition	.45 ACP
Total length (folded butt)	75.8 cm
(retracted butt)	75.5 cm
Barrel length	20 cm
Weight without magazine	4.65 kg
Weight with 30 round magazine	5.5 kg
Firing rate	Around 400 shots per minute

The M3A1 on which the handle type bolt handle, considered too fragile, was removed in favor of a simple hole in the breech enabling the weapon to be armed by using a finger. To facilitate this operation, the ejection port was widened.

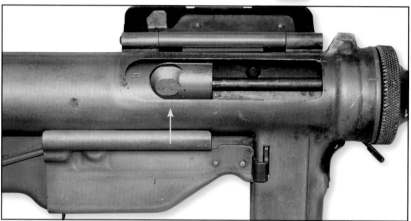

Detailed view of the M3A1 breech and its arming orifice corresponding to the size of a gloved finger.

A metal tipped casing was therefore added to the lever, without any change of name to the weapon.

Tests were carried out to equip certain M3s with curved barrels to make a weapon to "fire around corners" based on the model of the German *Sturmgewehr* fitted with a "*Krummlauf.*"

The Hi-Standard Company ensured the assembly of the Bell silencer on a thousand barrels pre-threaded at the muzzle and perforated with twelve series of four holes. These silencers were used during and after the Second World War by the Office of Strategic Services (OSS) and Special Forces.

In order to resolve supply problems in the zones where .45 ACP cartridges were not readily available, a unit enabling the conversion of the weapon in 9 mm Parabellum caliber was also put into service. The weapons converted in this way were fed by Sten magazines.

At the end of the Second World War, a copy of the M3 in 9 mm Parabellum caliber was made in China by the arsenal at Nankin. After the communists took power in continental China in 1949, this project was taken up in Formosa (Taiwan) where these 9 mm caliber M3s were adopted under the name M.39.

The few accessories of the M3 were:

* a canvas cover with a zip,

* a magazine pouch with three compartments for three thirty-round magazines,

* rubber caps to cover the magazines and prevent the entry of foreign bodies,

* a conical flash concealer which could screw on to the muzzle with a butterfly nut,

* a tool for loading magazines,

* a cleaning kit consisting of a chamber brush, rod, and rag holder.

Some M3 and M3A1 supplied after the war by the USA to France in the framework of military aid were used by the French army in the Algerian war.

The Ultimate Simplification: The M3A1

A simplified version of the M3 which was meant to remove the fragile bolt handle was the subject of a study from April 1944. The weapon resulting from this process was adopted in December 1944 under the name M3A1. On the outside this version is very similar to the original M3 from which it differs in the following areas:

During the liberation of Plouye (Finistere), August 28, 1944, an American soldier holds two German prisoners in a Jeep with his M3. *US Signal Corps*

- the lower block no longer has a bolt handle.

- the ejection port is longer than on the M3 and an orifice, drilled in the mobile breech, meant the breech could be moved rearward with one finger to arm the weapon.

- the circular base of the barrel has two flat-spots which facilitate screwing and unscrewing. The parallel branches of the butt can be used as a key for unscrewing.

- the clamping spring, to slow down the unscrewing of the barrel, is slightly lengthened to reinforce its action and to make handling easier.

- the shape of the butt plate is modified, so that this part can serve in the loading of magazines.

- the oiler, positioned on the right side of the M3 receiver, is removed: it is the cavity formed by the interior of the pistol grip which serves as an oil flask and its base is closed by a small screwed cap.

- the magazine catch is strengthened.

During the Second World War, 646,000 M3 and M3A1 submachine guns were made by Guide Lamp, a division of General Motors.

A second contract for the manufacture of 70,200 M3A1s was passed by the US Army during the Korean War with Ithaca Gun Co. Inc, which in fact only made 33,200 as the contract was terminated early due to cessation of hostilities.

The M1A1 barrel (right) bears two lateral flat-spots to facilitate unscrewing, if necessary with the help of the butt braces used as a collet; the barrel of the M3 (left) does not have this.

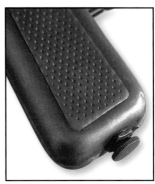

On the M3A1, the oiler housing has been removed and the grip contains an oil reservoir, the cap at the base has an applicator.

An M1A1 sight; a single eyepiece pierced in sheet metal. Note the concentric circles around the eyepiece which create an anti-reflective surface.

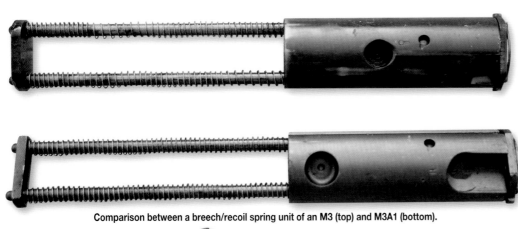

Comparison between a breech/recoil spring unit of an M3 (top) and M3A1 (bottom).

Comparison between a trigger-guard on an M3 and an M3A1.

All parts on M3 and M3A1 submachine guns bear a stock number: a modern arrangement, designed to make the management of spare parts easier. The initials "GL" can be seen indicating that this trigger guard belonged to a weapon made by the Guide Lamp company.

M3 DISSASEMBLY

1) Press magazine release button

2) Remove magazine from weapon

5) Press gun stock release button

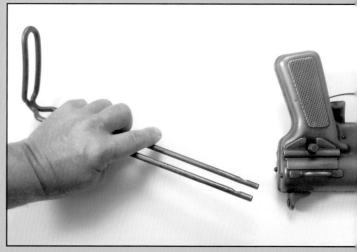

6) Remove stock

9) Depress the barrel ratchet

10) Unscrew the barrel while depressing the barrel ratchet

11) Remove the housing assembly

3) Open ejection port cover

4) Put the bolt in rearward position and check the absence of cartridge in the chamber

7) Disengage the trigger guard by inserting the butt of the stock inside and pry the guard outside the assembly

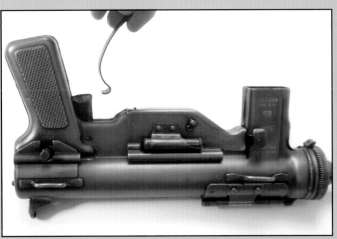

8) Unhook the trigger guard from the housing assembly

12) Open the cover, and withdraw the bolt and guide rod group from the receiver. By removing the springs from the guide rods, the bolt can be separated but this is not necessary for field cleaning

A disassembled M3 submachine gun: we can see the very small number of pieces as well as their large size to prevent loss in the field.

US M3 cleaning kit. The rod, formerly in brass on the Thompson submachine gun, was conserved, but it was now in parkerised steel either with or without a brass tip. This photo shows a chamber brush and spare parts bags supplied for the maintenance of US regulation weapons.

Soldiers often went on patrol with two or three magazines assembled top to tail with adhesive tape, so as to be able to reload their weapon rapidly.

gty.im/
3270485

Par Keystone

Test of an M3 fitted with a curved barrel based on the "barrel that can shoot round corners" (*Krummlauf*) of a German 44 submachine gun. *Thomas B. Nelson*

M3A1 with curved barrel. *Thomas B. Nelson*

Magazine pouches for magazines for US M3 or US M3A1, the canvas is less rigid than on the equivalent Thompson magazine pouches.

M3 fitted with a Bell silencer used by OSS commandos. *Thomas B. Nelson*

M3 and M3A1 flash concealer.

M3A1 barrel made by the sub-contractor Marlin.

CHAPTER 6
THE REISING SUBMACHINE GUN

Eugene Reising was the assistant to John Moses Browning in the 1900s; he had taken part in the development of the automatic pistol which was adopted several years later by the American Army under the name "1911 model." His experience with Browning, joined with a passion for firing and several years spent in the ordnance of the US Army, naturally led him to conceive his own weapons.

These were initially hunting rifles as well as pistols. In 1938, Reising became interested in submachine guns and attempted to design a weapon both easy to make and accurate, which would be likely to answer the demands of the army if the political situation in Europe was to continue to worsen.

He presented his finished prototype to the Harrington & Richardson Arms Company of Worcester, Massachusetts, in 1940. The company showed interest and bought the manufacturing rights to his weapon. The first Reising submachine guns, christened "model 50," left the assembly lines at Harrington & Richardson in March 1941.

Unsuited to combat in sandy conditions, the Reising showed no operational problems when it was used at sea. One of these weapons can be seen in the hands of American sailors guarding the crew of a recently captured German submarine. The show of force used to watch over a few unarmed men seems to amuse the captives! *DR*

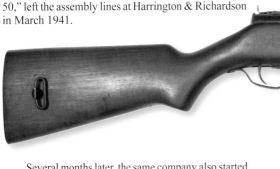

Reising model 50 seen from the right. *Collection of the Royal Army Museum of Brussels, photo by Marc de Fromont*

Several months later, the same company also started to make a compact version, removed of its firing compensator and fitted with a folding butt in metal wire stock: this was the 55 model. Later a semi-automatic version with a slightly longer barrel than on that of the model 50 but with no compensator and cooling flanges was also made under the name "model 60" for civilian use.

Principally made from pressed parts, the Reising fired from closed bolt with a delayed blowback and has a separate striker (non-pivoting, sliding hammer) which hit the firing pin when the gun was discharged. The delay for opening movement of the bolt was provided by displacing its rear upper edge from the recesses, made on the inside of the receiver. Its bolt handle was positioned in a cavity machined under the handguard.

Harrington & Richardson proposed their submachine gun to the US Army who subjected it to a series of tests at Ft. Benning, Georgia, in November 1941 (one month before the Japanese attack on Pearl Harbor). The deterioration of various parts interrupted the tests and Harrington & Richardson had to then present their weapon again several months later for a new evaluation after correcting the defects. During the course of this new series of tests, carried out at the firing test range at Aberdeen, Maryland, the submachine gun was rejected for presenting two firing incidents out of 3,500 shots fired (one of the incidents however was attributable to a faulty cartridge).

The receiver bears the name of the company Harrington & Richardson who ensured the manufacture of the Reising submachine guns. *Collection of the Royal Army Museum of Brussels, photo by Marc de Fromont*

Characteristics of the Reising M50 and M55	
Caliber	.45 (11.43 mm)
Ammunition	.45 ACP
Total length	90.5 cm (78 cm for the M.55)
Barrel length	28 cm (26.5 for the M.55)
Weight without magazine	3 kg (2.8 kg for the M.55)
Weight with 20 round magazine	3.7 kg (3.4 kg for the M.55)

Reising model 50 submachine gun seen from the left. *Collection of the Royal Army Museum of Brussels, photo by Marc de Fromont*

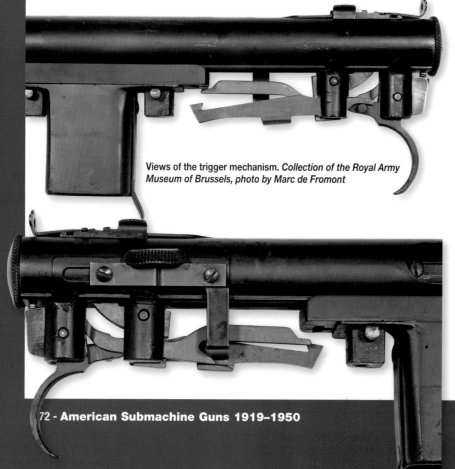

American soldiers and their Reisings with folding butts, in the jungle on the island of Bouganville.

Views of the trigger mechanism. *Collection of the Royal Army Museum of Brussels, photo by Marc de Fromont*

Lack of Reliability

As the United States entered the war against Japan and Germany in December 1942, the Navy and Marine units feared their men would not have enough submachine guns should they be engaged in land combat, as the production of Thompson submachine guns was at that time monopolized by the land army.

These two units, who benefitted from a great independence concerning the purchase of their equipment, therefore ordered Reising submachine guns directly from the Harrington & Richardson Company.

Initially, the buyers of these weapons were attracted by the Reising as it was lighter and better balanced than the Thompson, moreover its accuracy in single shot fire was superior. The general staff, for their part, appreciated both its immediate availability and its price ($62 for a Reising as opposed to $200 for a Thompson). Finally the existence of a version with a folding butt was particularly appreciated by the parachutists of the Marine Corps.

The weapon was used in combat by the Marines at Guadalcanal and by the Marine Raiders and Paramarines when they carried out reconnaissance on various neighboring islands before the main landing. The weapon was also used during the combat to recapture Bougainville, and the Reising was used by the Marines who came to reinforce British troops stationed in Iceland in 1942, to prevent German troops from gaining a foothold in that country.

During their use in these various situations, the Reising proved to be sensitive to the entry of foreign bodies into the mechanism and, to prevent the risk of jamming, their users had to make every effort to keep the weapon extremely clean which was often impossible for the units landing on the Japanese-occupied Pacific islands.

The disassembly of the weapon for cleaning in the field was difficult. The badly positioned bolt handle was difficult to maneuver and the user was often obstructed by the sling, which got between the user's finger and the bolt handle. The sight which had no protection was easily distorted and the foresight often lost because of the accidental unscrewing of its maintenance screw nut.

At Guadalcanal, the commander of the first detachments of Marine Raiders ordered his men to throw their Reisings into the lagoon and to get equipped with Springfield 1903 rifles which had a proven reliability. As soon as the Thompsons were available in sufficient quantity, the Reising was relegated to second place; used for training or transferred to the Navy and to Coast Guards who found them suited to service on board ships. In these conditions, as the weapon was not exposed to the possibility of sand entering the mechanism, they showed no particular operational problems.

Reising submachine gun along with a tropical helmet of the US Marine Corps, and other American equipment from the Second World War. *Collection of the Royal Army Museum of Brussels, photo by Marc de Fromont*

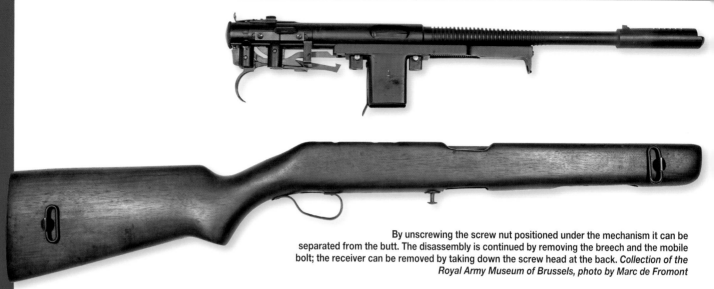

By unscrewing the screw nut positioned under the mechanism it can be separated from the butt. The disassembly is continued by removing the breech and the mobile bolt; the receiver can be removed by taking down the screw head at the back. *Collection of the Royal Army Museum of Brussels, photo by Marc de Fromont*

Later on, the Reising was also allocated to Canadian and British forces. Some of them took the place of the Thompson as weapons on board vehicles sent to USSR and this is doubtless the explanation for the fact that the Reising appears on foreign weapon identification files of the Wehrmacht under the name "MP 762 (r)."

The sight is of a fairly rudimentary manufacture, as is the rest of the weapon. *Collection of the Royal Army Museum of Brussels, photo by Marc de Fromont*

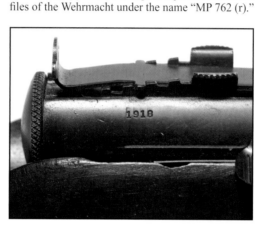

The bolt handle is positioned in a cavity machined under the handguard. *Collection of the Royal Army Museum of Brussels, photo by Marc de Fromont*

The manufacture of the Reising submachine gun was stopped at the end of the war. The total production is estimated to be in the region of 120,000, two-thirds of which were bought by the Marine Corps.

Harrington & Richardson also manufactured a semi-automatic rifle using the same mechanism as the Reising and this was called the "model 60." The Ministry of Defense brought several hundred of these weapons at the end of the Second World War to arm the guards in charge of protecting weapons manufacturers against acts of sabotage by Nazi agents. After the war, the Reising model 60 pursued its career as a police weapon. Its manufacture carried on until 1949 but commercial sales were insufficient and it was stopped after 3,000 weapons of this type had been made.

After the war, many Reising weapons downgraded by the Navy and the Marine Corps were brought by the US penitentiary service and police forces.

In 1950, the demand for this model by the forces of order persisted and Harrington & Richardson started production again up to 1957. Around 5,500 weapons were made during this period. They are distinct from earlier productions by their bronzed finish (instead of being parkerised as the war models were), their fixed gunsights, the absence of sling rings, and their barrel presenting twenty-eight cooling flanges instead of fourteen as on the war model. Their serial numbers were preceded by a capital letter indicating the year of manufacture.

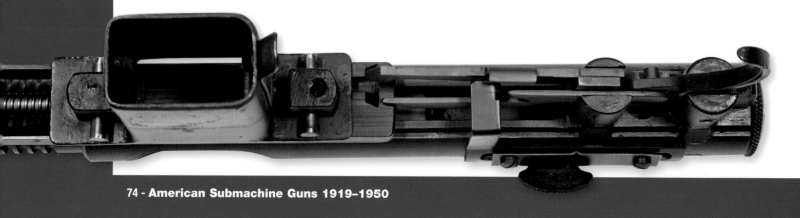

American soldiers in the jungle on the island of Bougainville, armed with M1 Garand rifles and in the front row one of them is armed with a Reising with a folding butt.

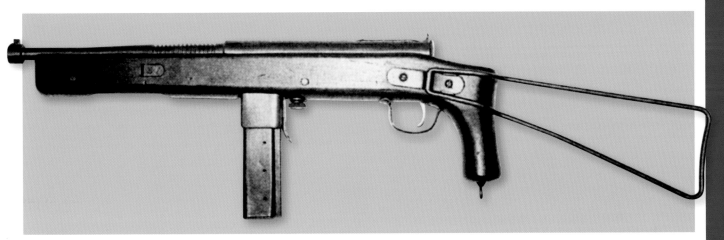

Reising submachine gun in the folding butt version particularly appreciated by parachutists of the Marine Corps.

When Harrington & Richardson stopped manufacture, the Numrich Arms Company of West Hurley bought the spare parts remaining in stock and created a small series of Reisings for sale to collectors. These weapons are recognizable by their serial number preceded by the letter "S" and by their butt plate in plastic bearing the Harrington & Richardson mark (the military models of the Second World War bore an unmarked steel butt plate). Their magazine catch is made in a single piece and the edges of the bolt handle housing are less pronounced than on pre-1945 models.

The model 50 Reising was also used by various countries in Latin America and Africa as well as by the *Force Publique* of the Belgian Congo.

UD42 fitted with a double magazine, composed of two 25-round magazines welded top to tail.

CHAPTER 7

THE UD42

Just like the Reising, the UD42 was conceived and began to be manufactured on the eve of the entry of the United States in the war. The conception of the submachine gun itself is the work of Carl G. Swebellius, a brilliant weapons designer who was the founder of the Hi-Standard Company.

The mechanism of the weapon was patented in 1940. It was commercialized by the United Defense Corporation, whose headquarters were in New Haven, Connecticut.

United Defense (abbreviated to UD) was one of many companies set up in the United States at the beginning of the Second World War with the objective of selling military equipment to allied countries at war.

The submachine gun of Swebellius interested the Dutch government in exile in London who wanted to arm its colonial troops who were defending Dutch possessions in the West Indies. United Defense finalized an agreement to have 15,000 of its submachine guns made by the Marlin Firearms Company also of New Haven.

But once the order was produced, the Dutch Indies were invaded by the Japanese and the Dutch government limited itself to buying just several UD42 to arm the crews and the marines of the Free Dutch naval forces.

The remainder of the UD42 remained for a short time in the warehouses of the United Defense Corporation and the company tried in vain to interest the American Army in its weapon by having a .45 caliber prototype made and a short version without a butt.

American soldier with a UD42.

Characteristics of the UD42	
Caliber	9 mm
Ammunition	9 mm Parabellum (9 x 19 mm)
Total length	82 cm
Barrel length	28 cm
Weight without magazine	4 kg
Weight with 25 round magazine	4.5 kg
Firing rate	Around 800 shots per minute

UNITED DEFENSE SUPPLY CORP.
— — —NEW HAVEN, CONN.— — —
UD M.'42   PAT. APPLIED FOR

United Defense Corporation company markings.

The 9 mm caliber version seemed interesting for the young American secret service agents who were attracted by this weapon; easier to handle than the Thompson and which fired ammunition very common in occupied Europe. Eventually it was the Office of Strategic Services (the OSS turned into the CIA after World War II) which bought the UD42 submachine guns still available at United Defense, to arm the commandos and the resistance fighters acting behind Japanese or German enemy lines.

The OSS seemed to have sold a part of its UD42 stock to the British special services (Special Operation Executive, or SOE) who parachuted them to European resistance fighters (particularly in France) and armed SAS commando teams and at Jedburgh, sent to occupied Europe to instruct and supervise the resistance.

Presentation

It consists of a 9 mm Parabellum caliber submachine gun, firing with non-fixed breech. The breech has two cylinders: one of a small diameter which bears the ejector and the bolt head at the front.

The other is of larger diameter whose forward part has a cam at the bottom; this hits the rear of the chamber when the breech closes and thus activates the firing pin.

The cylindrical receiver is entirely machined. The eyesight is at the rear and has micrometric adjustment. The bolt handle and the ejection port are positioned on the right side of the receiver.

The uncovered barrel is screwed into the receiver and can be detached by yanking on the pistol grip attached at its lower part. This arrangement makes the weapon less bulky for transport.

Fire mode selector markings, also acting as a safety catch.

UD42 next to an Enfield revolver and surrounded by demolition equipment. The Enfield was extensively parachuted to resistance fighters by the SOE. *Collection of the Royal Army Museum of Brussels, photo by Marc de Fromont*

The UD42 carried two numbers, a fact which has intrigued collectors for a long time: the serial number stamped under the grip (here 10085) and under the chamber is different from the number (here 9980) stamped on the right side of the frame under the initials "UD." It is most likely a stock number of the user body.

The serial number under the chamber. The proof stamp "AN" can also be seen demonstrating the weapon has been de-activated and the welding point, preventing the unscrewing of the barrel, is also visible.

Entirely made of machined steel, the UD42 is distinctly different from low-priced submachine guns, such as the Sten, parachuted in great number to the resistance. This photo shows the moveable sight, the distance on the sight is adjusted by turning the wheel on the left side of the frame (arrow).

After lowering the disassembly lever positioned on the right side of the frame, it is easy to separate the recover from the frame and go on with the disassembly of the weapon.

The frame bears a fire mode selector on the right and ends at the rear by a half pistol grip butt whose butt plate has an oiler butt trap for the transport of an oil flask.

The magazine catch is situated at the base of the magazine housing. The UD42 is supplied by a straight 25-round cartridge which is a scaled down version of the 9 mm Parabellum of the 20-round magazine of the Thompson submachine gun. United Defense also proposed a unit composed of two magazines welded top to tail; which allowed the user to restock his weapon rapidly by unscrewing the empty magazine and carrying out a 180° rotation of the two magazines to present the full magazine in position. However, the lips of the reserve magazine, facing down, were exposed to knocks and dirt which eventually rendered this layout unreliable.

A handle positioned on the left side of the frame ensured the locking of the receiver on the frame. Two wide sling rings, one positioned under the butt, the other under the barrel (in front of the pistol grip) permit the use of all rifle slings in service in the American Army.

On every UD42 the serial number is stamped under the chamber and under the grip while a different number is struck vertically at the rear of the frame. The presence of both numbers raises a question for contemporary collectors: it is highly likely that the vertical number is quite simply a stock number stamped after reception by a user body.

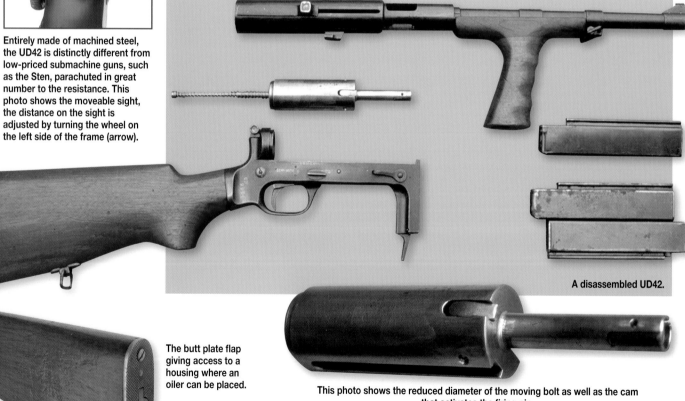

A disassembled UD42.

The butt plate flap giving access to a housing where an oiler can be placed.

This photo shows the reduced diameter of the moving bolt as well as the cam that activates the firing pin.

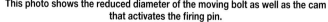

Marking on a 25-round magazine. This marking is no longer visible on magazines welded top to tail whose front sides are assembled by welding.

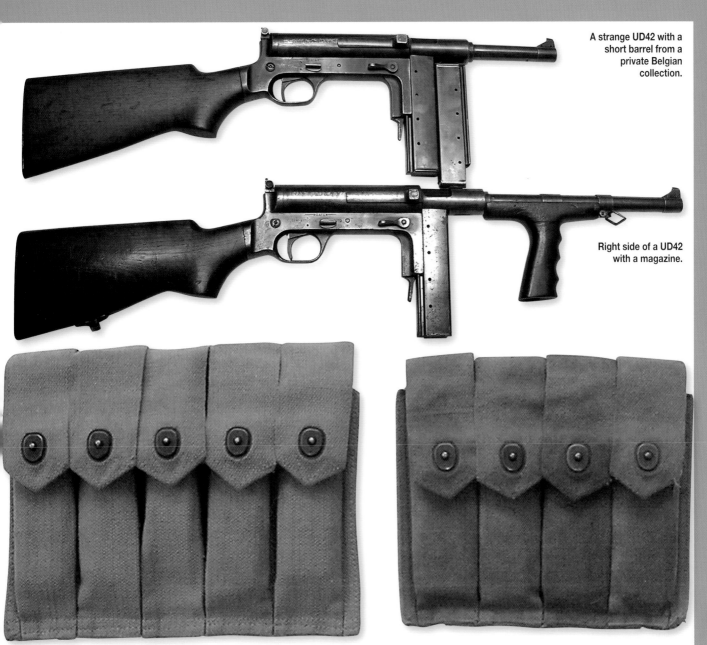

A strange UD42 with a short barrel from a private Belgian collection.

Right side of a UD42 with a magazine.

Comparison between a Thompson magazine pouch for five cartridges on the left and UD42 pouch on the right showing the difference in dimensions between the two.

UD42 magazine pouch.

SAS parachutists armed with UD42s somewhere in the Balkans during the Second World War. *DR*

German Submachine Guns, 1918–1945
Bergmann MP18/I • MP34/38/40/41 • MKb42/43/1
MP43/1 • MP44 • StG44 • Accessories
978-0-7643-5486-1

The Sten
The Legendary World War II
British Submachine Gun
978-0-7643-5485-4

CLASSIC GUNS OF THE WORLD SERIES